Writing Career Coach Press (a division of Writing Career Coach, 14665 Fike Rd., Riga, MI 49276) functions only as book publisher. As such, the ultimate design, content, editorial accuracy, and views expressed or implied in this work are those of the author.

Cover design by Zakr Studio www.zakrstudio.com
Author photo by Julie Dolen

ISBN-10 0983360766

ISBN-13 9780983360766

Jen Tucker

The Day I Wore My Panties

Inside Out

For Marge,
Lots of love to you!
Jw 2012

For Dana who wishes I would have chosen a word such as bloomers, knickers, underwear, loincloth, skivvies, drawers, jockeys, boxer shorts, britches, undies, corset, long johns, pantaloons, lingerie, bikini or thong rather than the one that graces the title of this book

For June, Eddie Lee, Lauretta, and Meredyth

Table of Contents

What people are saying . . .

"Jen has a terrific writing style, and is all too funny!"

> - Debbye Butler,
>   Author of Patient in Affliction

"I've been so there!" That's what women will say when they read, laugh and cry through Jen Tucker's The Day I Wore my Panties Inside Out. Tucker leads you by the heartstrings and funny bones through one day of her life that's filled with a husband flying off to Germany on business and leaving her to tend their three children, a butter-eating Golden Retriever, and a claims adjuster visit to their home that was flooded the day they moved in. Life lessons are expertly tucked in between each humorous take on Tucker's day. Her book dances with vignettes to which every woman can relate. Be prepared for tears when she writes of the wrenching love and protective ire she has for her misunderstood child with a motor plan disorder, yet laugh over her dry cleaning debacle. Sit back, chillax and read away. Tucker will remind you to "live above the stuff that life throws our way." And we all need to hear that.

> - Angie Klink,
>   Author of Divided Paths,
>   Common Ground

"I found myself nodding YES in agreement and chuckling to many parts of this book. I related to a lot of what Jen's book had to offer. I felt like as if I was sitting across from her at her kitchen table with a cup of coffee going over her experience. This is a relatable book with a personal feel few authors can accomplish and Jen does just that in a fun and beautiful way."

> - Gracie Soldani,
>   Author of Gracie's Orders

Salute

This is usually the place where you see that little word *acknowledgements* in the book you have just picked up. Sometimes you read them first, sometimes you read them last, and sometimes you ignore them. Honestly, I do all of the above depending on my fervor to dig in a new book and read; I get it. So you are not going to hurt my feelings if you begin this journey here with me, jump ahead, or this is the last of this section you read because you want to get to the goods! I have some things to say and to acknowledge people is nice, but that word just does not cut it for me. I acknowledge people in the grocery store. I acknowledge that I pay taxes every year. I acknowledge that if I do not get in there quicker than everyone else in my house, my shower will be cold in the morning. I rather like the word salute. That is what I want to do here; *salute*-to honor, to greet, to pay tribute. It's a verb and according to Schoolhouse Rock, it's what's happening!

I am forever blessed that I met Tiffany Colter who asked me if I would just send her a little something "chick lit" because she thought I was funny and had the most peculiar things happen to me. I sent it to her, and now you are reading the fruition of my whackadoo life that made her laugh. I am so thankful, Tiff, that you made me hop on the ride. Seat belts optional but highly recommended.

Willa Trethaway you brought a spirit of expectation that I humbly pray I lived up to. I believe in you as you believed in me. I still like you and you still like me. That's what it's all about! Thank you friend.

Kitty Eatherly has been my friend for more than 10 years. A friend who told me it was time to get off my butt and write again so she could get me out there for you to enjoy. Thank you Kit Kat for all you do for my soul and my calendar.

Many thanks to Debbye Butler who just could not contain herself and the track changes, and you know what? I am OKAY with that! I told you it takes a village to care for Jen Tucker and I was not kidding. Love you!

Rachel Smith, you are one of the women behind *the* woman! I am so glad that we share a love of appliances and Drew Brees.

As for my friends; I have some of the best. You fill my life and challenge me. I mean you *really* challenge me sometimes. You are the ones who understand that I am not worried about which one of you moved my cheese, but rather who ate my last peanut butter cup. And yet, you still love me.

I made some promises to a man at the altar at the ripe old age of 22, and as my parents were quaking in their boots, I knew I was marrying my soul mate. No one could ever fill my life with as much magic and bliss as you do Mike. Thank you for thinking I look hot even when I wake up with Flock of Seagull hair. Thank you for our three children, two dogs and a frog. Thank you for your integrity. Thank you for straightened paths and U-turns. Thank you for finishing my sentences. I love you.

For God who opens doors, knows the plans He has for us, and reminds us not to be anxious while waiting on their fruition. I know I ask You for a burning bush sometimes Jesus to lead my way in this life, but I really think that would scare the snot out of me. So instead, I thank you for all the other types of signs you leave for me that are not necessarily lit on fire. They are lit brightly enough when I choose to see them.

Something to Ponder

Four square was truly the only game that serious recess attenders played at my elementary school. No jungle gyms or basketball courts. We had a huge bin full of balls and a few jump ropes. If you got the ball out of the bin first at recess you automatically got the king square, meaning you called the shots. You made the rules. My favorite part of being king had to be the power of calling the rule of the "do-over." Do you remember the feeling of being able to call a "do-over" playing four square on the elementary playground? No one really questioned it. You could call it almost anytime you wanted to because someone had called it the play before. That is unless you had the rule of "no do-overs" which fell into cadence with the other rules such as no take backs, no double taps, no cherry bombs and the like. Just being able to replay the action as if nothing had ever happened was a gift. Like an eraser sweeping over the moment and leaving it to be replayed with the errors gone. Wouldn't it be just peachy if life was like that?

We have all had those days... be honest! I have them a lot! My friends and I often joke about the "do-over" and talk about how that would play "off the court" if it was a possibility. That will happen when you roost with a husband, three kids, two dogs and a frog. Some blame it on rising on the wrong side of the bed, the full moon, Nostradamus and his cohorts, but I think that it can be summed up into a simple four letter word. There is a very technical term for it that Dictionary.com defines as "the course of existence or sum of experiences and actions that constitute a person's existence." That defines the word when used as a noun. If you are talking adjectives, this word means "for or lasting a lifetime; lifelong."

The word we are talking about is **life**.

We live *life* daily regardless of circumstance and surroundings. We move through *life* moment by moment. Sometimes the path we take is not always the easy way traveled. Regardless, it is the direction we choose to move in due to that little gift called *free will*. Lives intersect other lives. We step into the lives of others every day; be it on purpose, on accident, on cue, on guard, or on faith. There are moments, words, and actions that you wish you could relive and replay. Just as we cannot put toothpaste back into the tube after we have given it a squeeze, hitting rewind with our diction or actions just isn't going to happen.

You can choose to live life riding the ever trustworthy merry-go-round which will never let you down. It moves in a cyclical and circular motion with predictability and safety. Merry-go-rounds never veer off course. There are still choices to be made on the merry-go-round. You either pick the horse that moves up and down very slowly and rhythmically, the horse that is bolted to the floorboards (and that baby is going nowhere), or you can rest on the bench that is stable, sturdy and your feet won't leave the ground. It's pretty safe on that horse that rises up and down once in a while. It's much safer sitting on the motionless horse, or the bench that never moves.

Why would you want the repetitive and predictable when you can hop on the roller coaster version of life? You buckle up knowing that the wind sweeps you around hairpin curves and dips that cause your stomach to shake hands with your throat. It is neither feared nor shunned because the momentum is welcomed and all it has to offer. I always think of the scene in the movie *Parenthood* where Steve Martin is visibly uncomfortable with the ride he is on pertaining to his family, career, and overall cards he has been dealt in life. On the other side of the screen is Mary Steenburgen who rolls with the punches and likes the hills and valleys of their journey together.

She embraces what rolls her way and she always knows that on the other side of the falling of tears are cresting smiles.

I want to tell about one day in my life. Well, there are a few days in there really, but the heart of the story centers around one in particular. Partake in the fly on the wall analogy and entertain just a few of the encounters I seemed to have been a magnet to. Please keep arms and legs inside the vehicle at all times!

A Moment's Notice

I want to introduce you to a term my friend Sheryl Lewis taught me a long time ago. It is the term **married single parent**. Let me start out by saying that this term *in no way, shape or form* can even compare to being a single parent. That is the toughest job on earth. Nothing could be more difficult. I commend all of you who are raising your babies on your own and making your family the light of your life every day. I truly mean that from the bottom of my heart. I have dear friends who grew up in single parent homes, and I have treasured friendships with single moms and dads today. I honor you and wish for you an unending amount of peace, patience, and Red Bull.

This term stems from family dynamics where mom and/or dad is traveling for work, yet one of you remains home to care for your family while the other is gone–perhaps gone a lot. I mean A LOT! Maybe you have a commuter marriage with you or your spouse gone during the week, then returning to be home on the weekends. Or maybe there are huge chunks of time where one of you has left the coop for weeks out of a month. It is a family structure that so many relate to these days. We live in a time where Momma and Daddy have to go where there is work. And that work just might take them far away.

My husband, Mike, has a job that takes him away many days every month. He works for a medical company and part of his commitment to taking care of patients is getting out and about and visiting doctors, hospital sites, and colleagues in the United States and abroad. That means he goes where the action is rather than the action showing up in our hometown.

Mike loves what he does and feels so thankful not only to have this job, but to work for a company that truly cares about people and patients in a time where the "all mighty dollar" can tend to rule corporate America. In his former life, Mike worked with his dad for many years at their family business. When you leave the place of employment where your name is on the building and the buck stops with you, there is a slight learning curve to entering the corporate workforce. Rather than a learning curve, I think it feels more like being in on a "secret handshake." Regardless, Mike has made the transition, and more often than not he is on the road, on a plane, onto another place. He loves it.

It is so funny how I find out about these trips he takes, because when you work in the field Mike does, they are not trips planned out months in advance. One day he is home for dinner at 5:00PM, and the next day he is a taxi passenger in Seattle trying to get to his hotel. It is strange for us to get used to this new way of life. It doesn't wean you in slowly; gently. No, no…the trips happen a little something like the following.

**Please note the role being played by my husband in the following scenario is that of Tuck. That is the nickname he went by during his years at Purdue University and that is what pops up when he instant messages me. I'm going to go by Jen Jen because that is what my friends call me and if I pop up on BlackBerry Messenger that is what you will see. I love nicknames. I have lots they are…wait, I digress. I am sorry but you might want to get used to that now because I will do it a few more times. Here we go…

Tuck: Baby are you busy?

Jen Jen: No, what's up?

Tuck: I'm going to Germany

Jen Jen: Really?!? That is so stinking cool!

When?

Tuck: Tuesday

14

Jen Jen: Tuesday when?

Tuck: Next Tuesday

Jen Jen: You mean Tuesday of next week?

Seriously?!?

You know today is Thursday right?

Tuck: Yep

Jen Jen: So you know that is T minus 4 days and counting right?

Tuck: Si

*Sidebar-Mike double majored in college and one of his bachelor degrees is in Spanish. The waiters love to chat with him when we go to Mexican restaurants; however they are convinced he is a cop. White bald guy who is fluent in Spanish seems to equal police officer no matter how hard he tries to convince them otherwise. Don't be fooled for he loves every moment of the mistaken identity. We have yet to receive free queso however. Oops, digressing again. I warned you.

Jen Jen: You know that is the first day the kids go back to school right?

Tuck: Yep

Jen Jen: You know I go back to work on Friday because that is when my school district is back in session right?

Tuck: Yep

Jen Jen: You know we are moving in the new house this weekend right?

Tuck: Yep

15

Jen Jen: I am sooooooo not ok with this bub! You are going to abandon me with a garage full of boxes, the first week of school for me and the kids, while the dogs freak out and probably lose their bladders and bowels in anxiousness all over the carpets because they live in a strange place now! Bob the frog will probably die and then I am the one who will be responsible for flushing him into fishy and frog heaven but wait I haven't even mentioned our children!!! I have to survive the kids trying to sleep in new beds with new sheets with new shadows that pop-up on the walls in the dark of night only to rise at 6am to get their booties on the bus and get Gracie to day care so I can go and save all the little people of the world at my job who need me and I just cannot believe you are doing this to me!!!! We still have not unpacked the flatware!!! I want to go too!!! Why can't I go!!! UGA!!!!!!

You know that is not really what I typed to my dear husband who has been given a tremendous and humbling assignment at work. It really went a little something like this:

Jen Jen: Wow baby! What a great opportunity for you. I am so excited for you ☺

Tuck: Me too!

I will miss you ☹

Jen Jen: I know, but we will be fine

Tuck: You are sooo amazing Blondie

Jen Jen: I know…It's not easy being me!

That is what I try to do when little wrinkles come my way in life. Notice I said *try*. Sometimes I freak out in my mind for just a smidgeon of time and then I am just fine and dandy. Those little freak-out mental moments do not happen to me often because I am the embodiment of the cheerleader personality. You know the type right? Do not sweat the small stuff. Life is too short. Everything you encounter should roll off your shoulders like water off a duck's back. Everything happens for a reason, and then in there somewhere is the girl power mentality. However, you will not find me in those Posh Spice stilettos. I have the worst feet ever. Bunions!

My glass in life is not only half full, but overflowing. Not so much with my dear soul mate. He thinks that the glass is not only half empty, but you shattered it while it contained the last drop of cola on ice with freshly squeezed lime, after you trekked across the desert with cactus needles protruding from unmentionable places because you fought off rattle snakes and their comrades for 40 days and forty nights. God definitely knew what he was doing when He paired us up. We complement each other and pick up in thoughts, words, and spirit where the other left off. I know…you are grossed out by how much we like each other already. Sorry about that!

Mike and I come from a place in our lives where we honestly feel we do not know the experience of real problems. When I speak of real problems, I am not talking about the times I forgot to pick up his dry-cleaning (there are several), or the times, yes *times*, that he shrunk my new clothes forgetting to hang them to dry (again…several instances). Those are not real problems! I speak to matters of losing love and faith in each other. Losing the desire or ability to communicate with each other. Losing a child. Those are real problems.

Have we struggled in our marriage? Yes.

Have we battled serious illness between us and our families? Yes.

Have we ever struggled financially? Yes.

Have we had to deal with serious issues with our children? Absolutely yes!

Our children are healthy. Our parents are both still living. We have a home full of the sounds of cartoon quotes, princess shoes clicking across the hardwood floor, and trombones played off key. Mike and I are deeply in love and have a beautiful relationship. We love our three children, two golden retrievers and Bob the frog. It's just that Mike gets to go to really cool places while I am the married single parent.

.

Just Take a Carry-on

The last time Mike traveled overseas was during his junior year of college at Purdue University. Mike was a double major, and has degrees in both Spanish and Restaurant and Hotel Management. Only upon showing his diplomas in three dimensional forms do Mike's friends truly believe that he earned two degrees. Not one he majored in and one he minored in, but two actual degrees. Before the proof in the pudding is revealed, most think that he just had a great time in college and has the six years of cancelled checks from his parent's tuition payments to prove it.

"Wow Tuck! You really did get two degrees!" our friend Kimi once said with utter shock dripping from her tongue while she eyeballed both of his diplomas.

"Did you think I was just screwing around for the past six years?" Mike retorted sarcastically.

"Of course I did!" Kimi said smiling through her teeth.

"Because normally, Tucker, we call graduates who survived six years of college Doctor!"

Needless to say when you are 22 years old, a male, and prepping to move overseas for a year to attend school in Spain, you are going to pack a lot of stuff, and I mean a lot of stuff! And the stuff he packed? In retrospect it made him, in his words, "stick out like the American Student sore thumb." He packed his

Nike's, his jeans, favorite cologne, stamps and stationery to write Blondie (that's me). The most precious item in his bag was his Discman. No, the most precious thing was his earphones that connected to the Discman to drown out the noise of Madrid!

Perhaps Mike's bags were fewer in number then and not as weighty as mine might have been if I was the one traveling for a year of studying in another country. That's probably true because he's a guy and I like a variety of shoe choices to accompany me at all times to most locations. Can I get an Amen? I was a Girl Scout, and Girl Scouts are always prepared. I have this ribbon at my parent's home (newspaper clipping to boot) claiming I won 3rd place in the city of Toledo, Ohio for The Girl Scout Cake Bake in 1980-ish I still feel, on my honor, the need to be prepared regardless of occasion.

But when you think about packing up your life and folding it neatly so that it will not become wrinkled during hours of flight and travel to Madrid, it is not an easy task regardless of male or female gender. It wasn't easy packing up my heart that left on that plane with him. Saying goodbye to my cute bartender boyfriend who caught my eye during the summer of 1992 was a tear jerker. We wrote letters. We had pricey Sunday and Wednesday phone calls. We made it work. 18 years of making it work to this day.

So we are now fast forwarding to 18 years post Madrid, and our life together remained mostly in boxes in our garage at this moment. We literally had just moved into our home a few days prior and I couldn't find a stinking thing! You know how you walk around like a zombie just praying to find the toothpaste? That was me. Why is it the kids can find the Xbox, the Wii, that shirt ripped and stained with the nastiest stuff on it that you swear you pitched a long time ago, but you can't find a dinner plate or your hair dryer? We found ourselves trying to get Mike all pieced together for his days in Germany, or Gern-a-mee as our four-year-old Gracie referred to it the entire time Mike was gone. It's a good thing he didn't need the hair dryer. He wears his hair a la Mr. Clean!

The joint was jumping with back to school jitters. I spent most of the day prepping the backpacks full of new school supplies with our boys Wil and Ryan for their first days of 8th and 6th grades respectively. Gracie as moving into the pre-kindergarten class at day care and I meticulously laid out outfits for Mike for the 9 days he would be away. I didn't touch a box. I did rock, paper, scissors it out with myself deciding I deserved a "pass" on unpacking.

When Mike got home from work, he told me he had several loving, yet strict, packing procedural lessons from the experienced travelers of the bunch. Many people that Mike works with travel frequently, constantly, non-stop. Those are the ones you want to take notes from. Heed their warnings.

"Jennifer told me I should be able to fit everything in a carry-on bag."

"You mean everything for work goes in a carry-on, and then you are taking the big suitcase right?!" I said puzzled.

"No, Jennifer, Bill and Silver all said I can fit 9 days' worth of clothes into my carry-on. That's the only way they travel and told me I should be wary of lost luggage so this would solve that problem."

"Are you serious Mike? I mean are you *really* serious because I do not believe them! I think this is the new guy going to Germany prank. I smell pranksters!"

"No baby, I'm telling you they only take carry-ons when they go overseas."

I could tell Mike was trying to reconcile it in his own brain as he talked to me about it. He was not even close to

22

sounding like a slick used car salesman. It was more like the young one who rings your doorbell selling you the school fundraiser goodies as they nervously shuffle their weight on their feet with knees knocking. I was not buying it. Not at all.

"So tell me this, you are gone for nine days right?"

"Right!"

"You need your suit with ties, dress socks and shoes and shirts for the times when you visit hospitals; khaki's and dress shirts when you tour the European offices and go to dinners; jeans and a sweater for cool days, and we haven't even covered boxers and socks and razor blades (Mike buys razor blades in gross because he shaves his head and has done so for the past 8 years)."

"Yeah…that sounds right to me Baby."

"There is no way! There is *absolutely* no way! Even if you did laundry half way through and took half as much, how in the world are you going to pack your suit in a teeny tiny suitcase without it looking like you accidently left it on the floor and the dogs slept on it? It is going to be wrinkled like crazy and who is going to press it for you?!"

Pause for dramatic affect as we stare at each other for a few ticks off the clock.

"Mike, I think they are totally pranking the new guy." I say this with the mom tone of voice. No man really appreciates that but it exits out my mouth that way regardless.

One more pause if you will.

"I'm going to text Jennifer."

"I think you should text her and ask her to come and pack for you because I have to see this for myself Mike! I'm not buying it!"

Off walks Mike into our bedroom, to text his boss Jennifer who is constantly on the go and traveling overseas as I sit on our closet floor staring at the surrounding hangers. I am telling you that I respect and find Jennifer to be such a warm and caring human being, but I smell some kind of initiation ritual here to torment Mike's packing, which in-turn radiates upon me 10 fold. I am asked to be the final inspection point before the suitcase closes, so if something is forgotten I put enough guilt on myself for the inconvenience Mike would find himself in.

I collect myself and then walk towards the end of the bed. Mike's phone chirps with the warning sound of a new text message. He then proceeds to read to me a "play-by-play" from Jennifer of how this is all going to go down. Tony Dungy could not craft an offensive route as clever and meticulous as this sounded. I think my eyes fluttered or I was distracted by a snoring golden retriever because I totally checked out during the lengthy packing instructions. I was a really bad co-pilot on this one.

Mike and I decided that he should get both the small carry-on suitcase and the large suitcase and see if indeed the smaller one was going to be "man enough" to get the job done. I was not going to be witness to this cramming of the business suit into something the size of a snack baggie debacle, so I went to check on the slumbering in our home.

I walked down the stairs and gently cracked Wil's door open. He was asleep somewhere in his mound of pillows. He is my teenage Olympian hibernator. We feel he could gold medal in the event and are currently looking for sponsors and perhaps some coaching to perfect his technique. He is the young man of the house. He treats me like a queen and his sister like a princess. Even though he is bordering the age of 15, when I watch him sleep I can still see him tiny inside of his crib.

I stepped out of Wil's room and walked over to Ryan's. He sleeps with his door open, so there was no creak of the hinges to wake him. I have no idea how Ryan could sleep in the endless orange ember glow of Pumpkin Toast paint on the walls. That is combined with the red lava lamp that is always on at night, erupting full blast. It's like a Hawaiian sunrise that stays constant at half-staff. I find it irritating, but Ryan finds it comforting. We let our children... NO! Mike Tucker let our children pick their paint colors for their rooms. I cannot forget the bedtime soundtrack that booms in this room. Ryan' stereo plays the Willy Wonka soundtrack over, and over, and over on the same song over, and over, and over. Why do children make musical taste mishaps when you spend so many moments; hours introducing them to a variety of cultures and classics in the melodic world? It's a crying shame. No offense Mr. Wonka!

Gracie was sound asleep surrounded by Valentine Pink walls. Proper nouns used here because that was the name on the paint cans. Remember when I told you Mike let them pick their paint colors? I tried to steer her in the direction of a softer, less eyeball punching shade of pink. No go. I even mixed up the paint cards trying to hide this lover's shade. Gracie kept finding it regardless of my sneakiness. She's crafty that one!

When I leaned over the bed to get a glance at her, she had her most prized possession cuddled up to her face and ever so slightly cresting over her lips and into her mouth. It was her blanket. She sucks on it. It's disgusting! It has gone by many names over the years, but she now has crowned it stinky pinky blanket. It is the grossest thing I have ever smelled. It is worse than those grease containers behind Chinese restaurants. I think the cure for the super virus can be extracted from this thing and turned into an antidote. She has three of these blankets and we rotate them after a good bleaching.

I was not going to be like my other friends whose children have a single one eyed bunny that cannot be washed or it will disintegrate, or one quilt tattered to bits that is held together by stitches, tape, staples and the like. No, we were going to have three blankets to make it less painful on us as parents to keep up with maintenance and repair.

SIGH

25

What we found by having three of these blankets is as follows: number one is usually in the laundry and would need to be sterilized by someone in a HASMAT suit, number two is usually hiding in the play oven or refrigerator and has been there for a very, very, very long time. The third blanket? It is likely seeking asylum in a distant land asking for diplomatic immunity. Tonight we were on the money and she was dreaming sweet dreams in the midst of the foul stench fabric she so treasures. That's my girl!

For those of you totally judging me right now as a bad parent, yes you, I want to tell you something. *I was you!* I would see my friend's children with their little lovey things and thanked God our boys never had a dependence on such items. *Oh my gosh! We left Teddy in the airport bathroom three time zones ago!* So you are going to let Teddy run your life? SUCKERS!

Then little Miss Tucker entered the picture and my judgmental self has eaten crow ever since. You do things with the third child you never did with the first two. It's survival mode people! You let them eat packets of sugar at restaurants while you wait on a tardy meal to be served. You let them have pudding for breakfast in the summer. You let them have a little more whining room. So back to this blanket issue. The dentist tells me that she is going to need braces regardless from the double face plant she performed one summer afternoon on a cobblestone walkway. So no "dental" excuse is excepted here to get rid of the blankets. Sorry! She will relinquish custody when she is good and ready.

I walked back up to our bedroom. Mike was reclined in bed watching TV. The large suitcase was packed, upright and ready to go. The small carry-on was unzipped and discarded. It looked like it might have been taken down in a back alley fight. I thought it might have a fighting chance when I left the room, but when push came to shove it was David with a broken sling shot against Goliath. I looked at Mike and was probably smirking because I just knew there would be no prank taking him down on my watch. Carryon bag…humpf!

26

The Day before the Day

I'm going to keep this chapter short because I do not like good-byes. I think that they stink. I had such a nice summer with my family even though there were events that kept us on our toes. This was my first summer off in many years since going back to teaching and working year round on my master's degree. Ryan was going to begin his middle school career today and I could feel how anxious and excited he was. Wil was already reminding me that Labor Day was the first vacation day of the new school year and wanted to make sure that it had a place of honor on my calendar. Gracie wanted to wear her Hello Kitty rain boots on the sunniest and hottest day of the week. Mike and I got everyone off to school and then he took me to breakfast. This was the first time that Mike was going to be gone longer than just a quick overnighter. I think my breakfast outing could have been guilt induced and I have no problem with that.

One of our favorite places on campus to eat is The Triple XXX. Let that soak in a moment and then get your mind out of the gutter. The homage is to a root beer that was created back in the day and subsequently, diners were opened across the states to market and sell the beverage. This is THE happening hot spot on campus, especially after a night of campus prowling and debauchery, for some good greasy food at 3:00am. A few years ago, the owners opened a second location named Route 66 and this one happens to be close to our home so we like to eat there frequently. This meal felt like the last supper.

Mike and I are rarely apart. We like going to the grocery together. We like spending evenings playing backgammon. We

28

enjoy being homebodies with our kids. Now that he travels, our time spent together is precious.

We are one of those couples that make people sick. We have been compared to the Buchman's (a la Mad about You sitcom in the early 90's), "the perfect picture of marital bliss," per our friend Fletch. I am not sure that it was said with admiration, more like the uncomfortable feeling of vomit rising in the back of one's throat. You might find that compatibility or bond with your sister or best girlfriend. I am blessed I have that with my husband.

Mike and I sat across from each other and really did not have much to say unless it was about the menu.

"Mike, are you getting the Drew Brees Special?"

"I don't know."

"I'm going to go out on a limb and get the Breakfast Special like I always do."

"Hmm..."

Exciting conversation huh? That was about all we could muster. I drifted away listening to the older couple sitting kitty-corner behind us in a booth. I heard him reciting a copy of *The Exponent*, Purdue's campus newspaper, to his wife. He was sitting across from her. She wore sunglasses with green tinted lenses. Her little yellow windbreaker over her shoulders, and he with his plaid jacket on. Both had walking shoes on their feet, that reminded me of my grandparents. The years had caught up with them, yet there they sat drinking coffee, enjoying jelly on their biscuits as he read for her words she could no longer see.

Moments like that get to me. Do you tear up at sappy Kleenex commercials too? When I see love lasting between a couple who have rode that roller coaster of life, I feel the commitment and promise they made to each other so many years before not knowing what would lie ahead for them. But there

29

they were. Together. In love. Reading the paper over biscuits and coffee.

"This really sucks!" Mike said after the hurried waiter took our order.

"I know, but at least we have email and cell phones and we didn't have either of those things when you lived in Madrid."

I was trying to reassure Mike as much as myself.

"Yeah, that's true."

More silence, followed by full bellies, followed by me taking Mike to work with his big suitcase where a rental car was to be waiting for him as his only companion to the airport. I felt sick. I really wanted to be brave, not the sobbing mess wife. *People do this all the time* I told myself. *Quit being a baby! Suck it up for crying out loud Jen! He's leaving for two weeks! He's not going to war! He's going to Europe!* I felt like my heart was leaving my body and taking a passport with it. He is my Edward Cullen for those who speak Twilight. He is my soul mate.

We embraced. We kissed. We said see you soon. I hate good-byes.

Butter Anyone?

We are rock steady!   There were no tears when I dropped Mike off, and I am zooming back to the house feeling pretty proud of myself I might say. Mike was at work prepping to leave for the next nine days, the kids were at school learning their little brains out, and I was celebrating a few more days of freedom before my summer ends and I head back to teaching. I am employed in a different school district than my children attend, which works out well to keep their humiliation of me being their mother to a minimum. The drama that would unfold if we cruised in the same hallways would just be enough to send them over the edge. To stay in their good graces, I decided to run home quickly, make a list of things to pick up for dinner and Bobby Flay my way into their good graces. A rule of thumb while Daddy is away is the path of least resistance is fine with me as long as no one ends up killed or in prison. If this means junk food for dinner one night, I am **okay** with that. We do have toothbrushes in our home after all people!

Not tonight though! Tonight I am going to cook for my babies and have one of their favorite meals for them to devour on their first day of school when they get home. I picked up a few odds and ends at the grocery and decided to make chicken swimming in olive oil, mushrooms, onions and garlic (hey…I'm not kissing anyone tonight obviously), mashed potatoes dotted with butter and blended with heaping amounts of salt and milk (no gravy necessary). No instant potato flakes! I'm talking about freshly cubed potatoes, slow boiled. Mashed potatoes like your

32

grandma had at Thanksgiving whipped into perfection. To complete the food pyramid, fresh green beans; slightly blanched.

As I made my way towards the front of the grocery, I was feeling really good about myself because I have left a window of opportunity open wide enough to go home and bake chocolate chip cookies. I wanted this dessert timed it just right. Making sure they were still warm and gooey when the yellow stretch limo, A.K.A. school bus, pulls in front of my house. I had left a stick of butter out on the counter to soften up and be ready for me to bake upon my return.

Who needs stinking Mike Tucker! Laugh! I'm sure you feel that way too. I am woman, hear me roar. I can be as much fun as Daddy. I can cook as well as Daddy; even better! *I am doing just fine and dandy on my own thank you very much.* The poor guy is going to be cattle prodded from gate to gate, and city to city over the next 24 hours, eating airplane food and trying to make sure that those seated around him know he does not enjoy small talk and making new flight buddies. I am sure they make a T-shirt or greeting card for that and if they don't, that is my new invention. Don't steal my idea!

I fiddled with my house keys, and as I nudged the door open with my foot, Jack and Henry were there greeting me with tails wagging and whimpers that had a tenor of "Gosh Mom are you home? Are you home Mom because we missed you when you were not home with us because you left us and did you know you left us and we were alone when you left us because no one is home Mom? Hi Mom, hi, *hi, HI*!!!!"

I am in love with our Golden Retrievers. We adopted them when they were two years old. They came into our lives at a time when I think we needed them as much, maybe more, than they needed us. We were a few months post losing our first dog. Theo was our "first baby," and came to us before our children were born. Cancer found him and it stole his energy, then his light, then his breath. Mike and I sat with Theo on the floor of the vet clinic the last few moments of his life. I will never forget stroking his head over and over craving to remember the texture

33

of his fiery red coat, the smell of his ears, his chocolate brown eyes looking into mine. Don't ask me if I have seen the movie *Marley and Me*. From what I understand, I lived my own version and it is too painful for this doggy mommy to relive. Even in big screen form. Many months later we were ready to open our hearts again. This time, it was twice over.

I tried to make my way through Jack and Henry, around them, between and over them to get my parcels from the front door to the kitchen. I plopped the brown bags on the counter and started unpacking. I noticed an empty, brown plate sitting near the bags. The same brown plate that was supposed to be supporting a room temperature stick of butter. Notice the use of past tense; *was*. No butter and two guilty mugs sat before me. Which of my four-legged children could pull off such a heist that potentially could rob young school children of a plate of love and tenderness after battling a day of middle school angst?

I will save you the suspense; Henry did it. How do I know? Henry has an eating disorder. Loosely translated means he eats everything and I mean *everything*! Well, that's not fair to say. He eats anything caloric that is meant to be digested by humans. If it comes in a wrapper, then that is just incidentals. He is the smart one. The calm one. The sneaky one. The one you would least suspect, and he played that card for a very long time until I caught him eating brownies out of a pan cooling on the kitchen counter. A few days after the brownie incident, I smelled his breath when a bag of peanut butter cup trick-or-treat candy was ripped to shreds across the family room. He failed the sniff test. It all comes down to the fact Henry has no poker face and never remembers to use mouthwash to hide the evidence.

Henry is a full blooded Golden Retriever. Jack on the other had seems to have a mixed lineage. Upon first glace you would think he is just a dog who is weight conscience unlike his brother. After you spend a little time with him you notice that he has some characteristics in his body type that just do not compute to make him a full blooded golden. He is very sleek and long, seems to have room to grow into his awkward feet, and if given just a small opportunity, Jack will run like the wind and just cannot stop no matter the tone of your voice or food item you bribe him to come home to.

His caramel blonde coloring and soft hair texture are the only shout out to the retriever family. We have batted around greyhound as a great grandfather, but recently my friend Julie threw afghan into the ring of potential family reunions. Maybe one day there will be a DNA test to quell the curiosity if Jack is related to the mailman's dog, but for now we just celebrate him being in our home.

He is our cuddlier; the biggest love in the world. His favorite spot to sit is on top of your feet. If you come over to my house and kick off your shoes, Jack is the feet-seeking missile. He finds the feet and plops right on top. He thinks he's a lap dog. A 100 lb. lap dog. Jack will lean into you with his entire weight, and also has a tendency to rest his head on any available body part. He is most fond of arms that are attached to hands that are trying to eat, or type. He purrs like a cat when he is content and being scratched in those hard to reach places.

"HENRY! WHAT DID YOU DO?!"

This phrase accompanied by the mommy tone of disappointment seems to transform my dog Henry from fun loving, chubby golden boy, to one I barely recognize. His eyes retreated. He squinted until no pupils were seen. Then he rhythmically serpentined his body towards the ground, into some sort of belly crawl, as if to say he could not feel any lower in life at this time.

He shows shame in a way only a dog can. Snakes could not have the ground to tummy contact Henry can achieve. Ladies and gentlemen of the jury, the evidence is staggering and the case is closed. Henry is a self-tattler.

So I hurriedly nuked another stick of butter in the microwave, which by the way does not mix into dough the same as softened butter that was left out on the counter. After putting groceries away and flashing Henry the look of death from time to time we are back in the cookie baking business.

I was cleaning up from the last batch baked when I saw the school bus curve towards our driveway. I quickly dried my hands and popped out the front door to wave in thanks to the bus driver who brought my boys home safely. I love watching the Tucker brothers walk up the driveway any day they return from school, but especially the very first one of the new school year.

In years past I would take a ridiculous amount of photos before school and after on this ceremonious first day. We would take photos posing by the front door, the group shot of all three children, and I loved taking photos of their feet. There was something about seeing their shoe size increase from year to year that just astounded me. I got the idea from a scrapbooking magazine years ago. I loved the idea of chronicling the changing, shifting sizes and styles. I feel as if we went from our first pair of baby walking shoes to men's sizes in a blink of an eye. And as the middle schoolers moved closer towards me, I felt the lump in my throat signaling to me that we have gone from action figure lunch boxes and superhero backpacks, to messenger bags and MP3 players all too quickly.

"Hi guys! How was your day?" I ask as I hurl my arm over my newly minted 6th grader's shoulder. I am promptly met with a Heisman trophy-like push off as my youngest son looks left and right to make sure that no one was watching and the bus has vacated the premises.

"*Mom,*" he begins in the irritated pre-teen tone. "Can you just wait inside for us to come in and then I can tell you about my day? I don't want anyone to see you out here hugging me like this!"

Pardon me?

"Ryan, you mean that you want me to wait on the front porch, or you want me to wait in the house? I don't understand and *why*?"

"We are going to walk up the driveway and you are going to wait inside. Wil, and I, will walk inside the house and shut the door. When you hear me yell, 'Hey Mom!' *that's* when you come down and talk to us about our day."

Wow...I think I just got voted off the island by my own tribal member that I birthed.

Wil had already gone inside by the time the berating was completed. Wil had always loved seeing me in the driveway after school and this year was no different. His younger brother had obviously reached a different epiphany about my presence.

Ryan is the same boy who put me on notice this morning that love notes in the lunchbox were to be a thing of the past (thank you very much).

"Mom when I was in elementary school I liked love notes in my lunchbox. You *don't* write love notes on a middle schooler's napkin. Okay?" He always looks like he is landing a plane when he speaks to me. Very animated arm movements. Meticulous hand maneuvering. Ryan gets that from me. Apples don't fall far from the proverbial tree so they say. God love him!

Thank God I can look forward to another little lunchbox to put my love notes in the near future.

Just as I relented to the love note thing earlier, I now had to promise to keep my booty off the driveway and in the house until my middle schoolers entered and then tightly shut the front door behind them. I was waiting for them to also tell me that the blinds had to be drawn. Heaven forbid someone be witness to me loving on them!

We walked into the house, separately and single file, and the aroma of warm treats met the boys at the door. The cheers I received instantly rebuilt my ego from the crushing blow in the driveway. I poured three glasses of milk and we began to compare notes about our days.

Life was interesting in the 6th and 8th grade hallways respectively. Wil took the lead.

"Hey Mom! Did you know that my friends and I figured out that we only have four years of school left and then we are finished...FOREVER!"

Uh-oh! How do I put this to him gently?

"Wil, you realize that you have to get through the entire year of 8th grade. That means you have five years left of school, not four."

It's a sucky thing to punch your own child in the stomach verbally. Freeze frame Wil's face and it showed he was on the receiving end of a hook, upper-cut, jab cross set of punches. Sorry first born son. So sorry!

Ry was next. Thank God I was allowed to actually have a conversation with him off the driveway! I was worried that was on the chopping block next!

"Mom I really like middle school! I think that Mr. Hopkins is going to be my favorite teacher. He is so funny! I didn't think that band teachers could be funny!"

"That's great Ry. You already have that figured out on day one?"

"Well I really like my math teacher too but that's gonna be a super hard class. Oh! But Jacob has science with me last period and so maybe that will be my favorite class…"

I listened intently. I soaked in the moments. I know that they will become fewer. I know they are fleeting. Just like love notes in the lunch box and hugs in the driveway.

I shared my story with the boys of shuttling their dad to work, but left out the detail about eating at one of our family's favorite joints. The major story was the grand theft dairy incident. Again I was cool in their eyes, and I am not ashamed to admit that I used some chocolate chip magic to get there.

Houston, we Have a Problem

"Oh man! I gotta run and get Gracie from school guys!"

"Mom, you're gonna be laaaaaaaaate," Ryan chided me.

"I KNOW!!!"

I grabbed a cookie for the road and dashed out the door.

You know how easy it is to lose track of time when you are belly aching laughing with your kids, best friend, a rerun of Seinfeld? Add gooey chocolate chip cookies and a frothy glass of milk to the mix and you will be late picking up your daughter from day care. This was her first week back after having the summer off. Moving up to the Big Kid's Room for my daughter was a big deal! She was so excited and could not wait to get back to school. Any parent that needs to entrust their most prized and cherished entity into to the care of another will tell that the ability to drop them off and not have a smidgeon of worry is the most amazing feeling in the world. Knowing that she loves school makes us happy. Knowing Gracie is loved deeply by those that care for her warms my heart to no end.

I walked in and saw Gracie watching *Lady and the Tramp* on the television with the handful of little ones left waiting for their ride home. I smiled when our eyes met. Gracie smiled back at me for a millisecond. Then her face contorted; serious face now. Laser beam gaze heading straight for me.

She got uppity.

"Mommy! Why did you come for me so late when I told you that I wanted you to come for me when it was after nap time and that is when the clock says three o'clock?"

You know those moments your memory lapses about your day? Did we truly have this conversation Gracie? Did I truly tell her I was coming after nap time at 3:00pm? Honestly Gracie, that happened? What else did I space that happened today? Did I stop the car at that four way stop sign driving here? Have you seen my purse? Have you seen my brain? Is she doing the Jedi mind trick on me? I have no memory of said 3:00pm retrieval time.

She scolded me.

"Mommy this day was so hard and I needed you to come get me when I told you that you come get me!"

She teared up.

"Preschool was the hardest day of my life!"

SNIFFLE

She let 'er rip.

"I want to go back to my little kid room!"

SNIFFLE *COUGH* SNIFFLE* *GAG*

She got to the heart of the matter.

"I'm not smart enough for the preschool room and I miss Miss Barb and Allie Cat (her bestie Allie) and all my friends are in that room and Andrew kept trying to hug me today and I didn't want him to hug me and then I had to do seatwork and hold my pencil the right way and Addie can draw people on her paper and

42

I couldn't draw people on my paper and I just wanted to cry for you because I just can't do it Mommy because it is so hard in Miss Debbie's class and I was just sad for you but you came late! *You came soooooooooo laaaaaaaaaaaaaate!*"

Oh boy…

Gracie had reached maximum overdrive. She was a screaming hot mess. I scooped her up; her head resting on my shoulder.

"Gracie, I'm sorry baby. I don't remember telling you that I would pick you up early today. If I did tell you that, then I am so, so sorry sweet pea. Do you forgive Mommy?"

Her little head bobbed up and down, granting me forgiveness, and she worked to recover normal breathing.

I buckled her in and she immediately stopped crying. I think there is magic fairy dust in my van.

"Mommy? Umm, can we listen to Rachel Yammi-gotti (recording artist Rachel Yamagata)? She makes me feel better when she sings and I need to feel better. I had a real tough day!"

I fiddled with the iPod and found Gracie's long distance dedication to herself. The first three tracks of Rachel's album Happenstance were loaded. Hit play. Cranked up the tunes. By the time we had left the parking lot and hit the main road, she was signing. Laughing. Talking about the great moments of her day. I *know* there is magic fairy dust in my van.

"Mommy, Andrew had his name on the board with marks after it. You get marks after your name if you are not a good listener the first time."

43

"Mommy, Miss Debbie has a tisket tasket basket that she puts her show and tell in. She tells stories about the stuff in her basket. Do we have a tisket tasket basket? I think it would be fun to have one like Miss Debbie's!"

"HAPPY PUPPIES DOCTOR!!!"

That is what we chant every time we pass my friend, Lisa's veterinary clinic. It's a race to see who says it first. It would be where our "happy puppies" go for check-ups, sleep overs when we leave town, and dog spa appointments. Getting 100lb a-piece golden retrievers groomed and not doing it yourself? Priceless!

Speaking turned to singing. Gracie did the singing, I was the attentive audience. If I sing, I get asked to stop. Not because I make mirrors want to shatter, or I can top a high pitched cat screeching. Gracie likes the floor to herself. She is a solo artist.

We were half way home, just passing the horse farm. Her little vocal cords booming.

I keep waiting for the day when Gracie realizes there is meaning in the words she sings. She'll ask me the thorough interview questions about love, relationships, heartache; the tough stuff we never want out children to face but know that they will. Doesn't it hurt just thinking about it? Be still my breaking heart.

"Mommy?"

"Yes baby."

"It was okay that Allie was not in my class because I saw her after breakfast and then we played at recess and in the gym too so I think that I will be sad that I cannot sit with her at circle time and I cannot sleep by her at nap time but when I get to see her all of those other times I will be so happy and it will be special and she is still my friend."

"That's exactly right baby! Allie is always your friend no matter whose class you are in. I am so glad you know that."

Awe! She figured out a life lesson all on her own; my little Gracie girl. Allie is still her best buddy even if they couldn't be together all day, every day. Gracie was going to embrace all the moments they had together rather than be angry or bitter when they were not together. That is a mucho important character trait to take into adulthood.

I know that you have a family with needs, demands, and the union contract hours to prove it. You have commitments; work, church, volunteering, sleeping, showering, feeding said family from time to time. You have the stuff that life brings you; illness, bills, emergency carpool duty, that 6th grade band concert that suddenly pops up. Five minutes before said concert, your 6th grader tells you that he volunteered you to bring snack. That's just the surface stuff of our lives right? There can be deeper things going on in your life that you might need time to reveal to the masses. I personally do not wear everything my heart and spirit are struggling with on the cuff of my sleeve for all to see.

Everyone knows someone who instead of being happy to see you at stolen moments, they immediately persecute you. Making it your fault that life gets busy. We all get busy. Not cool. Not cool at all. Let's leave the "mean girls" in middle school shall we? Take a lesson from Gracie Tucker. When one cannot sleep next to you at nap time, or sit by you at circle time does not mean that you are unfriended. So smile and enjoy the moments you can be with your gal pals. Bitter is unbecoming!

Gracie headed through the front door with blonde, stringy locks following behind her. She immediately greeted her "Happy Puppies" (her 100 pound a piece Happy Puppies) with love and hugs as she kicked her shoes off her feet. I am always amazed at how one shoe goes one direction and the other flies opposite. The first one she worked off without unbuckling it and it went straight up in the air. The next shoe, same technique but different on the follow through. Rather than it heading vertical it goes diagonal and lands across the dining room. How does this happen?

"Henreee, oh Henreee he's a babeee daaaaawg!" Gracie sang at the top of her lungs as she made her way through them to get to the kitchen for snack. She paused; startled. She sniffed the air. Is my daughter the only one with super human smells or do you have one like that too? She was a bit off today. Her sniffer usually kicks in before it hits the front door!

"Mommy? What smells good? Did you make cookies? Oh Mommy you did make me cookies! Thank you Mommy! Thank you so, so much for the cookies."

Wait for it. It's coming...

"Mommy, you are the best mom *ever*!"

Ah...thank you. Thank you very, very much.

My daughter is brilliant because she answers her own questions. Her woman's intuition is amazing, but more importantly she is the spawn of a chocolate lover. I've never met a chocolate I did not like except for white chocolate. What *is* that?! It cannot even really have membership rights into the chocolate family can it?

Gracie sat down with me and once again we broke dough together just as I had done with her brothers earlier. I love my daughter to bits. She is as mischievous as the glint in her eye suggests. She has that little sticking out of the tongue action that Michael Jordan had when he would try to "chicken-wing" a defender. He'd pop that tongue out of his mouth and go for the lay-up with rarely a foul called.

You know how when you were little, you would do some overzealous thing like paint your father's car with neon spray paint to save him a few bucks rather than have someone do it professionally and your mother says,

*"I hope you have a child **just like you** some day!"*

Uh-huh. You know what I am talking about! Here's the thing I don't get. I have one of those children that you're overburdened, sleep deprived mother wishes upon you but the omen for me remains the fact that I was NOT one of those kids! I was a great kid. A phenomenal daughter and I will say so myself!

"Ask Jenny Herrick to come over. Ask Jenny Herrick to go on vacation with us. Is Jenny Herrick going with you to the movies? She is such a nice girl."

When I came home I told my parents how lucky they were to have me for a daughter because the stuff *my* friends were doing was a million times worse than anything I had ever done in my life (not necessarily true, but my point was taken as such).

My daughter is Mike's "mini-me." He was a sneaky kid who got away with lots of shenanigans because he learned early how <u>not</u> to get caught. His sisters say that he was lucky, but my beloved prefers to attribute it to his mad skills.

Ladies, you will understand this mother's lament. Why do we spend nine months of our life knocked up, going through pregnancy only to have a child that looks *nothing* like you? They decimate our bodies only to birth these little balls of love that are born looking nothing like us, but everything like their fathers? It

47

leaves no paternity questions in our home. However just a little something that resembles my side of the family in their features would be nice.

They are peas and carrots, Mike and Gracie. They are Pete and repeat. Gracie is Mike Tucker in a dress with long blonde hair and girl parts. In fact, I make it known that the blonde hair and girl parts are the only thing my daughter and I seem to have that are alike. Gracie and Mike are so akin, that many times they butt heads, and I have to stand in the middle and referee. I send both of them to opposite corners of the ring, make them spit in buckets and shake hands before using their words again when the bell rings. Oh but how they love each other. Truly, she is Daddy's little girl.

"Mommy! Did you make these cookies for me because I went to big kid school today? Oh Mommy you are the best mommy ever and I just could kiss you lots like Dippin' Dots!"

"I did make them today Gracie. Just for you and your brothers. The first day of school is always something to celebrate after a long summer vacation, and I really, really missed all three of you today."

I tousled her hair from in front of her face so it would stop trying to sneak into her mouth with each bite she took.

"Gracie, how is it that you are getting more cookie on your face than in your mouth?"

She just laughed at me. I'm not sure how it could constantly happen; being the daughter of a chocoholic, but more of the cookie seems to go around her mouth rather than into her mouth. I do not understand that on any level.

By the time I started dinner it was closing in on 6pm. I guess I should mention at this point that I started cooking later than I had anticipated, so my menu changed just slightly. Before going all Julia Child in my home, I went upstairs and put on my comfy clothes. That usually consists of yoga pants, a t-shirt and my pink fuzzy slippers. The only thing that ever changes about this uniform is sometimes I wear little white athletic socks when I feel especially sassy. Who am I trying to kid; I have feet the temperature of an iceberg and I need all the covering my feet can get.

The kids were all occupied and so I went to work chopping and dicing, cutting and sautéing. The chicken swimming in olive oil and all the accoutrements became chicken swimming in instant onion soup mix. Mashed potatoes were replaced with instant rice, and rather than take all that time to ready the fresh green beans, we went with frozen mixed veggies or "mixed-up veggies" as my Gracie Lou Who likes to call them. My kids were none the wiser, however if they only knew what could have been, I might have been placed under house arrest!

We all sat down to dinner and *that* is when it happened. They came unglued. The spark explodes into flames. Why pour lighter fluid on a spark when you can dump gasoline?

This is how I wish the dinner conversation would have flowed:

"Gracie could you please pass me the salt?"

"Ryan, I would be more than happy to do that for you because I love you."

"Wil, at your earliest convenience, would you mind terribly if I troubled you for a napkin? I would hate to spill the delicious meal onto my school clothes that Mom and Dad so graciously bought for me to look my best at school?"

49

"Ryan I would be more than happy to do that for you because I love you."

In perfect cadence, my children would say, "You are the best mom ever and we love you and will devour every bit of food because you worked so hard to make us this nutritional meal. We will clean the dishes, put away leftovers and tuck you into bed Mom because you are amazing and we are lucky to be your offspring. Mother, we will not take no for an answer."

That so did not happen. It went a little something like this.

"Oh Tuckle (AKA Gracie)…"

"Ryan, don't call me that! MOM! Ryan just called me a Tuckle Buckle."

"No I didn't Mom! Gracie stop making stuff up and don't tell lies!"

"I don't lie Ry Ry, you lie when you keep calling me those words all the time so stop it, *stop it*, ***STOP IT***!"

"Gracie you are such a Tuckle Buckle."

"I told-ed you for the last time; don't…call…me…a…*Tuckle*…***BUCKLE!***"

Meanwhile, my oldest is chowing down and is somewhat oblivious to the whirling dervish that is surrounding him; until now that is when Ryan went after him next.

"Wil! Quit chewing with your mouth open!"

"Ryan, you're not the boss of me so be quiet! Mom, tell Ryan he is not the boss of me."

"Ry Ry" Gracie chimed in, "you don't tell my Wil what to do and you are a big meanie head! Mom, my dinner is yuck and I can't eat it because I am scared of this kind of chicken. Can I just have chocolate chips to eat for my dinner?" Ah, the logic of a four year old.

I took just a moment, a self-imposed timeout if you will, and counted to ten. Not slowly mind you, but lightning round speed. I was about to lose it. Nothing gets under my skin quicker than when mean words are hurled about between my kids. What *is* this dinner scenario? Are we filming *Jersey Shore* in my kitchen? I have lived with these people, my children, for several years now. They know how to instantly irritate each other. It is at times like this I understand the bliss my parents maintained by keeping me an only child.

I really should've waited to speak. There is a reason our momma's tell us to think first before we talk right? Before words left my mouth consciously, they definitely left without permission; I stood up from the table and somehow began channeling Joan Crawford.

"WHAT IS WRONG WITH YOU PEOPLE?!! NO ONE TALKS! NO ONE SAYS A WORD! NO ONE DOES ANYTHING BUT EATS IN SILENCE! YOU ARE ALL SO UNGRATEFUL THAT I MADE COOKIES FOR YOU AND COOKED A NICE DINNER FOR YOU! LEAVE EACH OTHER ALONE!!! DO YOU UNDERSTAND ME??!!!"

Right on cue the phone rings.

"I'll get it for you mom" Ryan says.

"You just sit down and I'll get it *myself*!" I said seething. I wasn't about to give a pass to Ryan's attempt at sucking up for a dinner gone tragically wrong. The caller ID displayed Mike's cell phone number. Great! Now I have to calm down and put on the nicey-nicey wifey voice. I can't have him hear me freaked out on the first day he is gone! UGH!! Why couldn't it be the magazine subscription schlepper calling so I could just ignore it?

I waited a second or two before picking up. Breathe in. Breathe out. Out with the bad. In with the good. Think cheerleader. All is well. All is great. All is calm. All is bright. I was really trying to get my heart to stop pounding in my head. I was so mad that he had left me alone with these people. Gracie sitting with arms folded and pouting; death stare towards Ryan. Wil and Ryan burning holes through each other with the same laser beam glares Gracie pulled on me earlier when I was a so-called "late arrival." I sighed. I paused. I faked a smile in my voice.

"Hello!" I turned on the sweet as pie voice so as not to tip Mike off to the ugliness at dinner.

"Hi baby. I just wanted to call and let you know I'm on the plane and heading to Europe. Baby, you won't believe it but I'm in business class! They are just bringing appetizers around before they give us a five course meal. I'm telling you this is absolutely amazing! I have my own TV, and I can choose from all of these different movies to watch. It's like my own personal Netflicks! Honey can you hang on a minute because the stewardess is bringing me a warm, moist towel? Hold on just a sec."

Silence on my end. I had nothing nice to say so I chose to say nothing at all. My mom taught me well. My mind had a lot to say however…

You ate a five course meal Mike Tucker with little tiny appetizers served to you? Gracie said I made scary chicken! You are in business class? WELL I AM IN HELL!!! You have your own TV? Well aren't you just something special! But let's not forget Netflicks at your beck and call… I HAVE A DVR FULL OF OLIVIA CARTOONS ON MY AGENDA THIS EVENING!!! Sure…sure I will be happy to wait for you to talk to

a leggy blonde stewardess with a 20 year old body, and perky
never breastfed a baby boobs. ***I AT HOME IN YOGA PANTS.***
I AM SCARRED FROM CELLULITE AND
STRETCHMARKS FROM BIRTHING YOUR LINEAGE!!!!!

GOD! That felt good!!!!

"Ok babe I'm back. Do you know what they just gave me? My own small dop-kit and there's so much great stuff in here! There's a sleep mask, earplugs, toothbrush."

"Huh! How nice to be sitting among the privileged."

"Wow! I really thought that this would be the worst flight ever because I remember flying coach to Madrid last time I flew over seas, but this is the life!"

"It sounds like you are living the life that Robin Leech reports on baby. I cannot even relate at this moment in time."

I did not marry a stupid man. Evidently this means I rock at masking dripping sarcasm that projects as true interest in anything else he has to say at this moment.

"We are going to take off soon but I just wanted to tell you that I love you and the kids and I will try to call you tomorrow morning. I miss you and I love you."

"Have a great flight Mike, and I love you too."

We said our good byes. I tossed the red, cordless phone to the counter. The children I had cesarean sections for, which I tell them means I was sawed in half and they owed me for that, were all giving each other nudges and dirty looks. Momma says don't speak, so don't speak!

Here I was in my kitchen, with these three children, wearing fuzzy slippers and glorified sweats while the man of my dreams was being spoiled rotten in an airplane. Nowhere near any of these three children.   Being served a multilayered meal by gals who were treating him like a king with perfectly rolled French twist hairdos. Dumb Germany! Stupid Netflicks! Stupid, dumb first class!

The Day has Arrived

It's a brand new day and boy was I thankful! While tucking my children in bed the night before, I had a serious talk with each of them about how we had to be a team while dad was gone. We had nine more days to survive without Daddy, and we had to stick together and call ourselves "Team Tucker!"

I constantly tell my children that "I am only one Mommy!" which usually signals them to cut me some slack and be kind to me so I do not crack under the pressure of their needs and wants that seem to be heaped upon me all at the same time.

Ryan helped Wil pack his lunch. Wil helped Gracie find her Hello Kitty rain boots to wear to school (no, it was not raining), and Gracie helped Ryan to remember his backpack. Who are you people and what have you done with my children?! Did you evict the crazies that had dinner with us last night and replace them? I *like* you. I like you all very, very much!

(Regardless of what you have done with them, you nice bunch of small ones may now stay forever.)

The boys hopped on the bus, and soon I was leaving to drive Gracie to big kid school. I was relishing in the fact that this was my last fun day to be had before I started back to work on Friday. Today (Wednesday) – all about me. Tomorrow (Thursday) – all about finding the box holding my flatware hostage. Friday – nose to the grindstone!

Today I had a ton of errands to run and I was excited that my dear friend Margie was coming over and was bringing dinner along with her husband Jon. Margie (hard G, not soft) and I have been great friends ever since I was her student teacher as an undergrad at Purdue. We have had a connection that has lasted almost (gulp) 20 years. It is a beautiful thing.

Margie is my mentor for matters professional, spiritually and personal in nature. We teach Sunday School together and it is like reliving our glory days, without the longer and bigger hair I had back then (1993 – now you understand). I love her dearly and am so blessed to have her in my life. Margie cooks up some good grub and, even better still, she was going to bring wine!

I was getting ready to head out the door when my cell phone rang. It was a number that looked familiar, but I just could not place it when it popped up on my screen. I answered with my rote, "Hi this is Jen."

On the other end of the receiver was our claims adjuster for our home owner's insurance. I know that adjusters in the insurance industry can automatically become a target of hatred that wells up from the deepest springs of one's soul just because of their title. Let me tell you, I just think the world of ours. I truly do! He was so kind to us, explained very thoroughly what he noticed and why, and also what would be covered and what would not from day one. That continued until the end. There is, however, the relationship between contractor and adjuster that can become a little tense from time to time. You can't fix your house without a contractor (unless you married Carter Oosterhouse…he's so hot), and you cannot have money to fix your house without the checks from the claims adjuster.

You maybe are thinking at this moment, *didn't you just say you had moved in the house like four days prior?* I sure did, and I will be right with you on that issue as well.

It turns out he wanted to pop by and take more photos of the repair work that had been done to date to fix the damage and wondered if I would be around. We set a time and said our goodbyes. I was meeting my friend Cara for lunch that day for her birthday, so I made sure that his arrival was early enough to not interfere with birthday fun. I then dialed up our contractor on the phone to let them know that the adjustor was coming out. I didn't know if he wanted to be here, if it was okay that he took pictures, if there were any questions I should ask, etc. I am a novice at this kind of thing and totally uncomfortable handling it. But what was I to do since Mike was disembarking on another continent? So I put on my big girl panties and a coat made of confidence. It did not fit very well however. I think it belonged to someone else.

I promised you a bit of back story to bring you up to this moment. Here it is. Five weeks prior to this phone call, Mike and I were getting ready to move into our new home. A storm rolled in like no other had in many years and no one could have seen nor predicted what was to come. It was a setback, but it could have been so much worse and we counted our blessings.

We had bought our house at the end of June and wanted to take a few weeks to paint and make it our own. We moved into town so I could work on my master's. We roosted with my parents until our home sold in South Carolina. What we told them would be a quick 6 week stay turned into two year. Can you imagine? Moving home with a husband, three kids, two dogs and a frog? My parents thought it was bliss! Me...not so much. I am thankful they tolerated us, loved us and are still speaking with us to this day!

On Friday July 9 we were to be on the road heading towards North Carolina to spend time with dear friends of ours who had recently moved there for a new job. Many months after deciding to take this vacation, Mike and I had made plans to buy our house. Unfortunately grown-up common sense kicked in, and we thought it was probably a little wiser to tighten our belts and have sparse summer vacation plans and use the money for our home. We were incredibly sad not to go spend time with Storie and Mike. I remember at that time going back and forth over this whole money issue and thinking that we really could get away, yet still have ample money to put into our home.

The aftershock of the storm would tell us that it was not about the money spent on vacation. It was about being at the right place we were meant to be, at the right time. That decision was critical. If we would not have been home and had been sunning ourselves on the beach; the damage that was to come could have been much worse in the long run. The possible mold in a wet house for over a week? Can you imagine?

With the rising of the sun on Saturday July 10, Mike and my dad were up and at 'em and went to the storage facility. I was at my usual perch by 8:00 am painting at the house like I had been doing since the day after we closed on the house. Only a few loyal advisors had been allowed into my circle of trust when I was picking out paint colors for the rooms that needed sprucing up. I asked my friends, my husband, and even complete strangers at Home Depot for their opinion.

My closest ally was very good to me. That would be the Pottery Barn paint swatch book from the spring 2010 collection. It really listened carefully as I worked through my thoughts about tones and hues. Never spoke a negative word to me when I couldn't make decisions in wanting to go from a mossy green, to khaki, and then back to the mossy green for my kitchen. Its patience was infinite as I worked back and forth through the color wheel more times that I can recall. At times I felt all was lost and I was overwhelmed and needed to step away to work through personal frustrations. Yet, it never judged me! It welcomed me back without question to find a color solution. Not just for me, but for my beloved family. All the rooms to spring forth with color in harmony. Thank you Pottery Barn spring 2010 paint swatches!

On moving day I was finishing up our Mossy Green second coat of paint in the dining room. There were few doors that needed another coat of Vermont Cream (it's just fancy talk for white paint in all honesty). I think the clock hovered around early afternoon when the rental truck was not so carefully backed up into the driveway. Mike popped his head in the front door and asked if I thought they should start putting boxes in rooms. I thought for just a moment,

"You and Dad have been working so hard today. Just leave all that stuff up in the garage and let's start moving it into rooms tomorrow. It makes more sense to only bring in a few boxes at a time." Again, I am thankful for things that were not yet seen.

We worked the hours away with my father hanging doors back on hinges, Mike helping me with a second coat of paint. I could see the light at the end of a long tunnel. Tonight we would sleep in our own beds, with sugar plums or whatever dancing in our heads. We would wake in the morning, go to church as a family and then come home and have pancakes for brunch before opening boxes. Unwrapping the familiars of our life as a family that had been displaced into boxes for many years. I smiled as I replayed that vision over and over in my head.

I have no idea where the storm came from because sunshine and light breezes had dictated most of the day. Thunder rolled in the distance and then the lights went out. There is nothing like having wet paint in the house and fading daylight to lead the way. I stood in the sunroom, just off the kitchen, and looked up towards the skylights. This strange pinging sound bounced off the glass above me. The wind was becoming violently authoritative. The sound crackled through the house. I worked my way upstairs to the master bedroom to get a better view of the storm from our windows.

I stopped at our East-facing windows and scanned the backyard. The pinging I heard was hail bouncing its way from our roof, to the skylights in the sunroom directly below. It varied in size from mini gumball to giant jawbreaker and then some golf balls joined in as well.

Further East out towards our pole barn, the trees that divided our yard from the neighbor behind us were being oppressively bent by the wind in one direction with their tops grazing the ground. Suddenly they changed course and swayed in the opposite direction with tops brushing the ground again. I think it was right about then that I realized I just might be in a tornado, and being on the fourth level of a house during a tornado was probably not the smartest place to be.

I began to run down the stairs when I heard Mike scream for me. "Jen! Jen, where are you?! Water is coming in everywhere! I need you!"

I sprinted down the last set of stairs into the sunken living room to see my husband try to mop under the window frame and my father following along the waterlines moving along the ceiling and working a small trashcan so that it would catch them as they fell to the ground. Water was rushing in from the other window frames now as well as down the sides of the chimney. We drug furniture out of the way or onto the plastic tarps we had used previously to paint. It was raining inside our home faster than we could keep up. I dashed into the laundry room and grabbed a trash bag full of clean towels and clothing and tried to mold it into some type of sandbag-like water repellant. My fear and quick movements were competing against each other for a breath of air. I realized Mike and my Dad left the room. I never heard them leave. I only heard my heart race.

"Mike! Dad! Miiiiiiike!"

No one answered me. *Where are they??*

Water was running down my forehead; my cheeks. Not tears. No time for tears! Where is Mike? Where am I; am I still inside? Feels like outside, because I cannot believe that there is a ceiling between the skies dumping this amount of water and my body.

I ran up one level, carrying an end table with shaking muscles. Dropping it onto a tarp I caught a glimpse of someone out the window. Mike! God there you are! I knew where he was now. I needed to find my dad!

"Dad! Dad are you in here?" I ran upstairs yelling for him and spun around changing direction when he answered from the basement.

"Jenny I'm in the garage trying to find buckets; anything to catch water!"

Once I knew where they both were I could catch my breath for just a moment. While taking that breath, I looked upon what had happened in my home. Water, ankle deep in soaked carpet. Droplets of rain parachuting from the ceiling. Plastic containers spilling over. I couldn't keep up the pace of bailing. It was futile. I stopped.

I walked into the sunroom. The blinds were open and I watched Mike. He had ripped off his Colts Super Bowl winning T-shirt and was fighting the rain barefoot. Ground water was trapped close to the house between the landscaping and the swimming pool cover. But the ground water outside was not the problem. The falling drops were the ones inflicting damage. He was holding a snow shovel and wielding it in battle against the deluge. I was mad. I wondered where his brain was. I am hauling furniture. I am mopping floors. My biggest question:

In the beginning of July, in a home we had yet to move into, where the heck did he find a snow shovel?"

I started to laugh. I started to cry while laughing. I would not allow ugly crying though. Not gonna give in. Not gonna happen. And it didn't happen.

This whole scenario was too much to take. Surreal like living a crazy Judd Apatow comedy! My husband is shoveling water just because he can. I am inside battling buckets like

Mickey Mouse in *The Sorcerer's Apprentice*. No director said cut and no one cleared the set. This was my reality.

Thirty minutes after this storm began, it moved on. The skies lightened and pinky purple streaks lit up between soft clouds. It was eerie really. Black skies turning bright. Birds chirping and flitting about like nothing happened. Spring rain had filled the air. Usually I find that scent pleasant, but not this time.

We called it quits on the inside. There was nothing we could do now. We stepped outside to the front porch and saw that our neighbors began collecting outside looking at the damage. Trees were down. Limbs fell inches from homes and cars. What a welcome to the neighborhood right?

I was on my cell with the water restoration company. Mike was on the phone with our insurance agent and friend, Chauntal. I hung up and sat on the front porch steps. My dad was in the house taking photos. With no electricity the lighting was poor, yet he still snapped away. Mike walked up the driveway towards me. We are both phone pacers; we think clearer when we take a few laps while talking.

"...well I am so glad you are okay too. You don't rush. Be safe driving over and we'll see you when you get here. Bye."

He sat beside me on the porch. I didn't really have anything to say. Not sure what to say to him really. Unbelievable what we just went through.

"I just hung up with Chauntal. She is driving over to see the damage. She was downtown working the festival when the storm came through. She said her husband had to hold up a tent with a couple other guys to keep it from falling on them!"

"Oh my gosh are you serious? Everyone okay? Was he hurt?"

"She said glass shattered and things were flying everywhere so I can only imagine that people were injured."

As overwhelmed as I felt with what we had been through, I instantly thought of others. People downtown with no warning that this storm was bearing down. No tornado sirens ever rang that evening. People enjoying a Saturday festival with their families, then attempting to take cover in open areas where there was no shelter. My problems here seemed small.

Mike and I watched people stroll up and down the street. Pointing towards damage. Pointing at us. My dad walked outside to join us.

"Guys I'm gonna run home and check on mom and the kids. I want to make sure the house is fine and they are okay. Let's stay in touch. Let me know if you need me to come back. With no electricity I assume there is nothing else we can do tonight to clean up."

My dad assumed right.

"Tracy from the restoration company is going to call me in the morning and see if our power is back on," I said. "So there is nothing here for us to do. Chantal is on her way over. We'll come home after she leaves."

Did I just say home? I was home. I was at my waterfront property. My dad backed his van out of the driveway. Mike grabbed my hand.

"I'm sorry Blondie."

"Why are you sorry babe? You didn't do this?"

"I couldn't save our house from this. I'm so sorry. So sorry."

64

Mike began to tear up. His voice was fading in and out over the words.

"Why were you outside shoveling? The water was coming through the ceiling not from the side of the house! I was inside trying to stop it, moving furniture; do anything I could. Why did you go out there and not stay in to help me?"

He grabbed my face to look towards him.

"Baby there was nothing, *nothing* I could do inside the house to stop what was happening. I had to get outside before I started screaming at God. Why us? Why? If I didn't go out there and do something I was going to lose it."

"I tried to see if the gutters were clogged. They weren't. I went on the side of the house to see if I could throw a tarp up there, but the winds coming from the east drove the rain in directions it never flies and I couldn't get up there in that wind if I tried."

My anger and confusion with him morphed into understanding.

"All I could find was that orange shovel. I saw the water collecting around the pool and I just started trying to shovel it away. The whole time I was doing it I was screaming at God, I mean yelling, screaming! All your hard work painting all day, every day for weeks in there for nothing. It's ruined! What purpose does that serve? What is that about? I'm so mad Jen. Just so mad!"

The words I needed to hear. I got it now. I would even daresay he was bitter that this is what was happening to us. Mother Nature was raining on our parade and Mike wanted to know where our rescue was. Where was that ever present help in our home's time of need? He felt forsaken.

As Mike and I repeated our story in the days and weeks that followed, friends and neighbors cried as they listened. I found myself comforting *them*.

You see, by all purposes we could have been moved in and enjoying family time on this night. My daughter at this time would have been sleeping in her god-awful pink colored room and the water would have come in on her through the window above her bed.

My dogs would have been sleeping on the floor of the family room that ended up soaked in inches of water.

We should have been gone today, stretched out on a beach with our friends in the Carolinas.

We would have been a week behind in discovering the damage.

The scene I play in my head as we open the front door carrying in our suitcases and finding the aftermath is almost too much for me; even mentally. I know you can see it with me. The boys jonesing to get in the front door, and away from each other, after 13 hours in the car side by side. Way too much togetherness. Sleeping Gracie being carried onto the porch by Mike. Me fumbling with the house keys while swatting bugs away under the porch light. The door opens and as it cuts the plane of the room, it's not home sweet home I smell. It's something else that is not in the same league as lavender potpourri! That is what could have been.

Blessings abound in situations where others see catastrophe. You just need to choose to see them.

Hello Kitty Meets the Golden Stealth Bomber

I live with six males. My dear husband, my two middle schoolers, two four-legged boys and one with fins. I was always outnumbered in our home until the day Isabella Grace arrived. We had always wanted to have three children ever since Mike and I started talking about a family. Well, that's not accurate now that I think of it. When Mike and I first talked about children, he told me that someday he would love to hear the pitter patter of eight little ones running around. I told him that he needed to find another gal because that was just not going to happen with me. He asked me if I would negotiate to the number five and I never committed. When Wil was born, Mike and I seemed to settle in on the number three. Number three didn't make her arrival until the boys were ages 10 and 8 respectively.

It's funny because when I told my girlfriends that I was pregnant for the third time I was met with many responses. They ran the gamete. My opening line to all my friends is as follows:

"Guess what Mike gave me for my birthday? A baby!"

The following are the responses I received from some of my friends:

Vicki-"Awwwwwwwe! That's so sweet! Mike got you a puppy…"

Nancy-"What do you mean? Like a baby-baby or a something else kind of baby?"

Jocelyn-"Are you stupid? Your kids are in elementary school and you are free! What were you thinking? You had it made!!"

My favorite reaction is the one that I got from my friend Susan. I had stopped by school where she is a teacher and survived having both of my sons in her class. I said, "Guess what Mike got me for my birthday." and pointed to my belly.

Susan said, "A new belt?"

Do you see a trend here? No one saw this coming and no one could *go there* in their minds and fathom that I would actually be pregnant.

It was also followed by the traditional comments wondering if Mike and I actually did this on purpose, because did you know that no sane people have a baby seven years after their last child is born? From what I gathered, it almost seemed as if it would be forgivable if it were an accident. Alas, our little bundle was planned and it was no secret that I wanted to have a girl. I had always wanted one. I like girly stuff. I wasn't really fond of dirt or dump trucks or massive amounts of using a couch as a launching pad for endless energy.

I am a girly girl. I like girl things. I am high maintenance, yet on the lower end of a high maintenance person. I had always pictured myself in life raising three little blonde lasses all wearing purple gingham with perfectly parted braids in their hair, and we would sit and play tea party and paint nails giggling for hours on end. We make plans and God laughs.

I did adapt. I overcame the learning curve of testosterone and I think I can hold my own! I love my boys, and they are still quite fond of me as we enter the teen years (as long as I keep a

neutral balance in public not to embarrass them too deeply--
please refer to the first day of school bus incident earlier in the
book).

My boys tell me that I am THE best mom ever. That
might be mostly because I make them tell me that after I give in
to a whim or deep desire they have, but I honestly see nothing
wrong with a little personal affirmation from time to time. Even
if it is received through bribery. And my boys think I rock!
Here's why:

- ☐ I can speak fluent Mario Kart,

- ☐ I know the win/loss stats of the Colts and Saints,

- ☐ I make pancakes bigger than your head,

- ☐ I have played the longest marathon Uno games of
your life

- ☐ I will watch an occasional zombie movie with
them

- ☐ I let them dress like gym rats with the exception of
Sundays

I love my boys! I love every one of their boogers and
burps that have passed through the halls, or stuck onto the walls
of my home. I am living the fraternity house dream! All you boy
baby mommas know what I am talking about.

We told the boys that we were expecting a new baby.
Their prayers to the heavens granting to them their sibling of
choice came immediately. Like their mother, they made no
secret about their wanted gender that would soon grace our halls.
I think that children have the inside pulse to God's ear, and they
used that hotline in a big way. Yes I know it boils down to DNA
and the X and Y chromosomes; however my boys did not see
genetics that way and put the desires of their heart into pure faith
and prayer. Sitting bed-side each night with the boys lifting up
their petition to the heavens went a little something like this:

"Dear Jesus, please bless the sick and the sad, Nanny Papa (Nanny Papa are actually two people, my parents, but my children squish them into one by conveniently leaving out *and* which could be to save time and energy?!?), people who need God, people in prison, our teachers and friends. And most of all Dear Jesus, please give us a sister. If you give us a brother it will have to go live with Nanny Papa and we will visit it on weekends, so we need a sister. Amen!"

Here's another one:

"Dear Jesus, thank you for friends and teachers. Thank you for our teachers who don't give us homework. Please give us a snow day tomorrow (this prayer was said in April) so that we can stay home with Mom. God bless the Big Bridge (that would be the Mackinac Island Bridge). Most of all, Jesus, we ask you for a sister to live with us because we have enough boys in our house and Mom needs someone on her team. Amen."

They don't mince words now do they? They worked those conversations with God on overtime. My boys knew that they went straight to God's ear. These hearty prayers continued until the day of the big reveal.

Mike and I took our sons with us the day we had our ultrasound to see who was about to join our family. A brother or a sister. Earlier in the day I had several voicemails from friends who were very concerned about my awareness that this baby could possibly be a boy and were not sure if I, or my boys, had considered that. This is my favorite one:

"Hey Jen, it's Nancy. I just wanted to call you and make sure that you were okay. I know that you want a girl, but you know it might not be one right? Call me back if you need the biology refresher course."

I understood the Vegas odds in this scenario. It was 50/50 odds. I made sure I wore pink underwear and a pink shirt just so I wouldn't jinx anything.

In the waiting room, the boys were asking me all about the ladies with blossoming bellies and looking at all the newborns in pumpkin seats. My children had an aura of audience members on Let's Make a Deal who would be really mad if behind curtain number two was not the sibling that they thought it was. Once we got into the room and the cold jelly hit my belly, the ultrasonographer put the wand to my abdomen taking measurements and getting her bearings on our baby to be. When the first little blob appeared on the screen, Ryan burst out with, "Is that her girl parts!" He was so disappointed to hear it was just the brain, but in hindsight it was definitely *the* girl parts (as we females are of higher order).

The technician asked, "So would you like to know the sex of the ba…"

"YES!!!"

Poor thing didn't even get the chance to finish her question.

In the seconds between our resounding YES and her answer to the question at hand, my thoughts went bonkers. Oh my boys... Are they going to need therapy if I'm knocked up with their brother? If this sister was not meant to be would we all need family therapy? Ugh! God whatever is to be will be.

Even though it was a matter of light seconds, the wait felt like eternity. She paused for a moment and then said, "It's a girl!"

What happened next I could never make up in a million years…?

Ryan and Wil began screaming and crying. Not a whimper, not a small tear falling onto their cheeks; screaming and crying. You would have thought that Oprah just handed them keys to a new car! "You get a sister! You get a sister! You get a daughter!"

They each grabbed my face and looked into my eyes but no words came out, only the strangest of sounds that resembled a moan from the belly. The boys had hit the freak-out ceiling with the screams and wailing, so I asked Mike to take them out into the waiting room.

When alone with the ultrasonographer, I asked her if she had seen anything like that before. I mean, *that* was a phenomenal reaction! I was thinking that in my kid's minds, they believed that they had just won Powerball! Two siblings overcome with such joy for their impending sister.

"The only time I've seen people reach hysterics of that level is when they don't get the results they wanted," she said with a smirk.

So I guess there is a first for everything!

When Gracie was born and arrived home she wasn't as much fun as her brothers had anticipated. She cried. She slept. She pooped. Repeat.

I am not sure what they thought she would do, but I think that they had a different picture of reality in their heads than the reality they lived in. They still loved her and stalked her relentlessly, however I think they had visions of her being four days old and battling them in a game of Nerf guns, or telling knock-knock jokes to them while pounding glasses of Kool-Aid one after another. A high like no other; sugar and red dye overload! They wanted to hold her, feed her and rock her. They also yearned to teach her about cars and devouring Mexican food as soon as possible.

Eventually all of those things happened and with it came the whines of "Gracie is touching my stuff! Mom, tell Gracie to get out of my room! Mom, Gracie is jumping on my bed!"

Be careful what you wish for boys.

Gracie got a pair of pink with white polka dot Hello Kitty boots for her fourth birthday. I have never seen a female so in love with footwear in my entire life!

She wore them at breakfast with her jammies.

She wore them cuddling with the dogs watching television.

She wore them in the rain, sleet, snow and sunshine.

She wore them to school almost every day.

Wearing clothing with them was always optional when indoors and at home.

Today it was the latter…no clothing. Just boots and a pair of princess panties. The rear-end of her underwear was graced with the face of Ariel, the princess of the underwater world. Gracie was finishing up the rest of her breakfast and singing to me from the table while I packed her lunch. Jack and Henry wanted to go out one more time before we left for the morning. I wasn't going to be gone long, just a few errands before the insurance adjuster came. Since our move was fresh into the house, we had not yet set up a system for the dogs to meander around the yard and were taking the "Happy Puppies" out one at a time on the leash.

I always hang onto Jack's leash for dear life. He is a gazelle! We are not sure of his heritage like I told you earlier, but we know one side of the family is Golden Retriever and the other is not. He is very streamline and thin as a rail, whereas Henry is a little more round and roomy. Jack will take off like a bolt of lightning and run until he realizes that home and dog biscuits might be too far off. If you open the door an inch, he will run a mile when the wind smells just right. Henry on the other paw, follows us around the yard, but never strays too far. He might miss out on a stick of butter if he flees the scene.

Jack and I headed out first. He on the receiving end of the leash. I could hear Henry's tail hitting the storm door that I left open. His whining was piercing my ears.

"Henry, I am coming back for you in a minute! Your brother goes first! You will live! Just wait dog!"

I walked outside with Jack and as he sniffed the yard, I saw Gracie come to the screen door in all her Hello Kitty boots, and panty wearing glory. She had found the latch to the screen door and began to push on it and watched as well as listened to it click.

Click-click, click-click-click. Click-click-click-click. CLICK-CLICK- CLICK!!!

"Mommy, did you know that the door makes music when you try to open it?"

"Gracie, please leave to door shut and stop clicking it open and closed!"

"But why Mommy?"

I bent over Jack to straighten out one of his ears. Gnats were buzzing about.

"Because if you keep opening and closing the door Gracie bugs will…

CLICK-CLICK-CLICK

75

"GRACIE! STOP OPENING AND CLOSING THE DOOR PLEASE!"

And before I could tell her that the door opening and closing lets the bugs fly in and use our home as a Gas and Sip for all insects and their compadres, and she could accidently flick that little lever down on the side and lock me out with no way to get back in without coaxing her through the steps to unlock it, something flashed before my eyes.

A golden hued stealth bomber rushed right past me. I barely got a glimpse of it before it was out of site. Oh good grief! It was either my own personal close encounter, or the beginning of an adventure for a yellow dog that lives under my roof. It was the latter. My stupid dog made a run for it!

"Jack! Get back here now!"

No good. He was a goner. He ignored me. Could care less about me.

I closed my eyes, bit my tongue and began dragging Henry up to the porch. But Henry wasn't at the end of this leash. Jack was sitting next to me with those eyes of a smug sibling. Jack was at the end of the leash I was holding. The good son...gone! Jack seized the moment and gave me the look. The look of... *Hey! For once it wasn't meeeeeee!! Mom I didn't leave you but Henry did and I stayed because I wouldn't leave you and I know that I leave you sometimes but I smell things and I must run because I need to find them and roll in them because they smell good but here I am mom! I'm here! Is Henry in trouble and can he be in trouble because I am always in trouble when I run away. Oh goody he's in trouble!*

The dog that shot by me in a blaze of glory was Henry! The one who never strays and never leaves the yard had booked it across the street and was heading towards the blueberry farm! I

76

stood there in disbelief and watched as my dog on a mission to find those berries was looooooong gone.

By this time, Miss Hello Kitty, standing in boots and panties was outside next to me. Hands on her hips.

"Gracie, did you hear Mommy tell you to stop opening and closing the door?"

"Yes Mommy and I did stop it! Henry clicked it open!"

"Gracie I heard you doing it over and over again and now Henry is gone eating the neighbor's blueberries!"

"Mommy, but I am telling you that I had stopped clicking it and was sitting at the table eating my granola bar when I saw Henry bonk the handle with his nose. He did it lots and lots of times and then BAM! He got it open and ran out the door!"

Her recollection of events, and lack of wardrobe – hilarious. The explanation of the events that led to our escapee was too much for me to take in. I bit my lip to keep from decimating her little ego and her quite serious explanation with my smile and laughter. She was so stinking cute!

Gracie and I stood in the side yard and watched for Henry to come home. I was not chasing that dog. I saw where he bounded off to. Plus my "shotgun" Gracie was inappropriately dressed for neighborhood gallivant. One of us was fully clothed and the other was missing a few items.

Henry finally returned after about a 5 minute walkabout at our neighbors farm, literally right across the street, and Gracie gave him enough of a scolding that I said nothing.

Could he even take Gracie seriously looking as she did? Three quarters naked on the front lawn, with her straggly blonde hair whipping about in the subtle breeze. Isn't it hysterical that my panty and boot wearing babycakes was shaking her finger at Henry? She was correcting him with quite a lecture as he fell to the grass, and then rolled onto his back in submission. I can't even get that old dog to do that new trick.

And so it was…Henry was smarter than the average bear and escaped the compound. Whatever the blueberry farm breeze blew into the house that day, it must have been too much for him to inhale.

He was driven, nay determined, to get to that farm. I shared with you earlier that Henry has an eating disorder. The disorder is he eats everything. And now the challenge before me was clear. Sturdy, strong, one million inch thick chain for the yard times two…pronto!

Speedy Delivery

After I dropped Gracie off at school, I ran to the bank. I think going inside of the actual bank must be a lost art. I am not fond of the drive-thru unless it is absolutely necessary. I have no idea what my ATM pin number is and haven't know it since my undergraduate years at Purdue. I needed it back then to score some green before heading to Harry's Chocolate Shop for an evening of laughs with friends.

I think it is important to turn off your engine, exit your car and actually walk into the bank. Don't you want to have some type of rapport with the humans who touch your money? Don't you want to "make nice" with them in-case of impending overdraft disaster? Don't you think they would be much more likely to cut you some slack and help you out if they could put your name with your face? Let's say, for instance, I might have written a check from the wrong account. Perhaps I closed that account a long time ago but still seem to hoard old defunct checks for some odd reason. Not that I would know anything about that. Remember – hypothetical!

I think it is imperative to have a presence with the people in your life that make your world run smoothly. I liken it to TSA at the airport. No, seriously, I do.

I know that you have been witness to it. The adventures in traveling gone wrong. You witness a duel between a passenger and a member of the TSA. It is the one traveler who feels like they can take 'em John Wayne or John McClain style and the only thing you are thinking is, *Buddy, if you keep me from getting to my gate on time, I am telling you that I will be your worst estrogen nightmare!*

80

No bag search is going to happen on their watch without a Hatfield and McCoy-esque adventure. These rookie passengers become put-off when they have to remove garb that seasoned travelers know you *never* wear through security lines. A sweater dress with a built in shiny, metal belt. Boots that lace up to one's knees rather than slip-ons. We all have stood in close proximity to such a traveler who did not plan their wardrobe appropriately.

And please tell me that, besides my best friend Nancy, none of you are the type to challenge the TSA. In Nancy's case it was an act of a woman who was trying not to be separated from her beauty products, and so she is exempt. You know there is that 3 ounce rule in a carryon bag right? Nancy, politely I might add, disputed the content ounces of her bottle and when she wanted to look for herself was scolded. Like my golden retriever was scolded for hunting for snacks at the local blueberry farm buffet.

She is also exempt for the sheer reason that when we were seven year old natural blondes trying to survive the remnants of the blizzard of 1978 outside Chicago in the grand city of Naperville. She helped me carry my smiley faced cupcakes to school as we walked to Highland Elementary over hill and snowy dale. These were my birthday cupcakes and their survival was of great importance.

Haven't I told you that story yet? It was a real sight. One of us would climb the massively high, grayish tinged snow drift and then hand over the precious cupcakes. Then the other would climb over the top and hand them back until we reached the next Grand Teton. This was repeated for a few blocks until we reached our destination. No one wants to see pastries die a horrible death in the middle of the street now do they?

Nancy and I both were admitted to Purdue University to attend college. One afternoon as I was watching the moments tick off the clock during a math class, I saw her wave to me in the hall through the open classroom door. I smiled, and gave a little wave back. A few moments later out of the corner of my eye I notice someone doing the wheelbarrow walk in front of the classroom door. Nancy had help from some strapping young thing who held her legs as she maneuvered her arms across the cold floors of University Hall. I started laughing and couldn't stop.

As she came around for a second pass, the jig was up and my professor stopped speaking and looked out the door to see my friend who looked like she was in the middle of a stupid human tricks audition for David Letterman. Professor glares at the entertainers. Entertainers apologize with "sorrys" wrapped in giggles. Classroom door closes. Boisterous laughter erupted from the crowd that had gathered to watch the spectacle in the hall who were waiting for classes to change over. The instructor walked over to me, stood in front of my decrepit desk and said, "Friends of yours?"

"Unfortunately," I stammered back wondering if this was going to result in some type of phenomenal punishment such as extra math problems being assigned, or a doctoral length thesis on proper classroom conduct even though I was not the conductor of the conduct. I was on the receiving end.

She turned and walked to the front of the class and went right back into lecturing on functions and equations without missing a beat. I did see our instructor's shoulders bounce a little seemingly working overtime to suppress some laughter. When class was over, Nancy was in the hall waiting for me and as soon as our eyes met we broke in to an explosion of cackles.

She is the friend who gets in her car very late on a Sunday night when you call hysterically crying. Telling her the news that your father has stage four colon cancer and you can barely utter the words through the tears and pain. As Nancy pulled into my driveway on that snowy January night, she realized she was missing something…shoes. In a rush to get to me, she'd run out to her attached garage sans footwear. It was just the laugh I needed.

Nancy is the friend that when my Dad's cancer returned two years later and invaded his liver, she sat with my mother in the waiting room of the hospital. I had succumbed to a raging

82

stomach flu that kept me away. I was devastated not to be there for my mom and my dad. From a childhood playing Barbies, to college wheelbarrow bedlam, Nancy has been there. I know you have a friend like that too.

You now see why I would have to stand with Nancy and defend any amount of illegal content in her carry-on that could possibly be considered oversized in the eyes of the government who is worried that her 3.0111 ounce lip gloss is a safety hazard to others.

In all seriousness though I must say this; I do not understand picking a fight with the TSA for the simple reason that they let you go bye-bye on a plane. They are the gatekeepers to your destination. Now, if you antagonize them, you run the risk of a super friendly pat-down, or never arriving at the place you were trying to get to. Is it really *that* important if they open your suitcase and rearrange your panties? Do you need to scold them? Is it really necessary to sigh and give dirty looks when they have to pitch your eight ounce sunscreen bottle because you did not check the label and do the math? Eight ounces does not equal three ounces my friend (once again-Nancy excluded because that one is all me).

We have a golden rule in place for a reason to do unto others as you would have them do unto you. It is accompanied by *turn the other cheek* because we are not always done unto as we would like to be. God made those rules for a reason. He foresaw us in line behind someone at the airport and knew we would feel anxiety. He foresaw when we need to go to the bank and plead for mercy because we accidently spent a little too much at Target getting a fix from the clearance rack on our debit cards. He truly does.

After stopping INSIDE the bank and saying hello, making a deposit and yucking it up with the tellers, I popped into the grocery store around the corner. I wanted to pick up some more butter because it seems to be a precious commodity in my house if you have four legs, paws and are named Henry. While I was in the store I got an email from Mike. (I, of course, get email on my

83

phone. You never know when valuable e-coupons will arrive or there is a forward that will ensure that I win the lottery.) He told me that he was alive and well and driving with his companions on the autobahn.

I think at this time he was actually a passenger and not so much behind the wheel burning rubber. I knew that if there was an opportunity he would be James Bond-ing it on the open road topping out at whatever speed the odometer would allow. Mike also wrote to me about how he and his companions had just left a hospital site meeting with physicians and they were heading to a ferry to get to Denmark from Rostock, Germany to go to his company's European headquarters.

I emailed him back and told him that I was grocery shopping, for more butter, and that I would be home later and would write more when I got home.

That is when it hit me. How amazing is email? Seriously! I think we take it for granted because it is readily available and can arrive to our cellular phones in an instant. If you do not have a cell phone with email, then it arrives at your home computer or one you might use at the library and never needed a stamp! Mike is in the northern tip of Germany, writing to me while travelling in a car on the autobahn. I was in the aisles of a grocery store in Indiana replacing the murdered dairy items and we were physically an ocean, several time zones and a seven hour flight away. Even with all of that space between us, we were connected.

Last time we had an overseas relationship, if we communicated by mail it was snail mail and it took days to arrive and required mucho postage on each envelope.

When I think about my grandparents early years of marriage, email was not a word known to Webster's Dictionary. For my grandfather, stamps were difficult to come by when serving with the armed forces on a navy ship off the coast of Hawaii. Here we were in real time communicating as if Mike was at his office working his usual gig in the same zip code as me.

Think about how amazing that is! And just as I am fascinated and thankful for this technology to communicate in an instant, in some ways I also find it sad. Not only do I have a feeling that we have lost the generation who knows what a postage stamp is, but also I think that the postage stamp perished along with the wrist watch that my niece and nephew never wear. Why would they wear watches if their cell phones tell time? Why would I put a card in the mail, or write a check paying my bills and send it off thought the postal service when I can do both of those things online?

Penmanship is still important. It is not a "dinosaur technology" as a teacher in South Carolina coined it during a parent-teacher conference I attended.

Can I give you a little challenge? I would love it if at this moment you pictured someone who made a difference in your life and let them come to fruition in your mind. It can be anyone. A favorite teacher, your best friend who is on the TSA's most wanted list, someone that time and distance has caused communication to cease.

Perhaps it is someone who inspires you in an amazing way and you have never met them. A news story might have introduced you to a soldier needing a boost of confidence and caring from a warm greeting. Maybe you read in the newspaper about a family that had suffered great tragedy and you were moved hearing about their struggle. Grab a pen and notepaper and send them a letter from the heart. Believe it or not, pens and stationary are still available at many fine and local retailers.

Life moves pretty fast as I recall Ferris Beuler saying, and as a result there can be unfinished business leaving you with the haunting question; what if? No one wants to live with that over their head. Do not live your life with any "what if's." Small ones, big ones. Rise above both of them.

My small what if's are just that. Small. What if I would've tried that new dish at Little Mexico instead of my go-to

85

Nachos Supremos (creature of habit)? What if I didn't have photographic evidence of my 80's fashion mishaps? What if I would have gone down the bypass and not taken the side road, because now I'm stuck behind a school bus stopping at every house. What if I would have seen that new romantic comedy and not this shoot-em up movie Mike wanted to see; I can NEVER get those two hours back in my life!

My big what if's are huge. What if I truly was there more for Nancy who lost her infant son instead of wallowing in my own insignificant problems? None of my problems were significant compared to hers. What if I would've listened to my gut when it dictated that Ryan get off the jungle gym rather than the afternoon ending with him in the emergency room receiving stitches? What if I would have called my grandmother when I felt the urge to do so and had the opportunity to speak to her the day before she died? That is the one that haunts me the most when I let it, but there are so many others. Some small and others of greater significance.

Do not let fear or pride keep you from discourse with others. Do not be afraid to try the new dish at the Greek restaurant. If you hate it, don't order it again. If you love it; bellissimo! Listen to your gut. It's that still-small voice alerting awareness. Do not let the hands of time tick by and then blame your lack of communication on busy-ness. Believe me I understand busy! I am trying to purge it from my life and I do not think that I am doing such a hot job at it most of the time.

I have this conversation with God a lot. When I feel overwhelmed and caught up in the dance of life I tell Him this:

"God, you know how in the original Christopher Reeve Superman movie Lois Lane got stuck in that huge crack in the earth? Lex Luthor, the self-proclaimed Greatest Criminal Mind of all Times, got the key codes for missiles and was playing a real life game of Risk with them and causes an earthquake? Remember how upset Superman was and he screamed out in anger and agony to the heavens when he was too late getting to

Lois and found that she had died buried alive in that enormous crack in the earth? Then there was that part where he flew up into the universe and spun the earth backward so that it was as if this horrible tragedy never happened and Lois Lane springs back to life with her car popping out of the earth at warp speed. Superman then swoops back in and finds Lois simply trying to start her car in the desert and saves the day; saves her.

I am very serious that I say all of this in its entirety!

The thing I am getting at is I would LOVE IT if you would simply spin the earth back a few revolutions so that I could get a few more hours out of my day. I do not feel as if I am being greedy because all I am asking for is two, maybe three hours tops! I am not asking for days or even years. Can you just help me out?"

I don't believe God is preoccupied with the box office or which movie in the Superman franchise I am talking about. If He did turn back the earth for me, would that truly help me learn to better manage myself and my time? Would that teach me anything about WHAT IF I was a better steward of my time? I should move quickly when I feel led by that feeling in my gut to do so. When I am honest with myself I realize that I have been given plenty of hours in my day. It is up to me to use it wisely and not squander it. I choose how I am going to make the moments count. I choose where I devote time. I choose what opportunities or moments will slip by in life and what will be important, and I am responsible for any of those that may one day turn into *what ifs*.

Part of my problem is that I am a *yes* person. Sometimes it is hard for me to say no, and I am not very good at it. It's not usually a problem to say no to an offer or outing that sounds like as much fun as a root canal trip to the dentist. It is much harder to say no to the fun stuff, and honestly why would you want to say no to it? That is unheard of and ridiculous right? No one wants to miss out on the action. We relish invitations to be included into social situations. There is a certain pride we find in being busy and sharing with others our overflowing, full schedules on the weekends.

When someone asks us how our weekend went, no one wants to admit that they stayed home and did nothing. But what is wrong with that? Why do we feel we need to keep ourselves in a crazed state of motion? Constant motion is not good for the body, the soul, or the family. I challenge you as I have been challenging myself to begin to really evaluate where you are putting your time and energy. Where are you putting your time as a family? I think you will find that much of your missing time can be regained in your day if you take control of your calendar and commitments and that it will not require the powers of Krypton.

The power I am most interested in using to my advantage to gain time in my day is finding a better place in my home to hide the butter. There are times I need to leave it out so it achieves room temperature and thus I will make less frequent trips to the store to replace it. The problem with that is if I find a new place to hide it from Henry and his butter sniffing snout, then I have to actually remember where I put the stupid stick and THAT is the problem. My fear is that I have the smartest dogs on the planet and if I write it down on a post-it note, Jack will put on a pair of Mike's readers and give Henry the location. They are crafty beasts. Do not put it past them…

Can't we all just Get Along?

I walked in the door and attempted to put my groceries away. The things that needed to remain cold were not the challenge, but trying to find the homes for the pantry stuff was. When you move into a new place you have this blank slate to work with. When the space begins to fill you realize that what remains empty is what you have to work with. Here's what runs through my mind...

If I put the peanut butter on this shelf in the pantry, then the kids can all reach it to make their sandwiches and get their lunches together for school. That means I have to move the bags of pasta that were there and in turn make a new shelf for pasta and rice, thus turning this peanut butter shelf into the kid's shelf so that they can have all of their stuff in one place and not mess up all of the shelves trying to dig for the peanut butter.

Does this shelf even have the clearance for the jar or is it going to be too tall and hit the top of the shelf above?

I honestly could get lost in it for hours and never before considered myself the "H" word. However, after a long conversation with my friend Michael, I have come to find out that I am... a food hoarder. I am self-diagnosed and feel like it is an accurate descriptor for me and my relationship with my consumable inventory.

I like to save certain things in my ingredient inventory because if I use it, then it will be gone and I will have to buy more. I do not want to buy more–so I save it. I cherish it and want to keep it around.

I have this bag of oatmeal and before I go on any further I have to tell you a little something about myself. I have Celiac Disease which is intolerance to the protein gluten found in wheat, rye, barley and sometime oats. I was diagnosed almost seven years ago and was literally at the end stages of it when we finally found out what was causing me to be chronically ill. So what does this have to do with oatmeal?

Let me put it to you like this. Nancy can buy a box of pasta on sale for 99 cents. Jen has to buy a bag that is much, much smaller and costs $4.00. Nancy could make a huge pasta salad for ten people with hers, and mine might serve just me. Nancy can buy Wonder Bread for pennies and when Jen buys a loaf of bread, it is half the size of said white bread and can be in the $7.00 range depending on the brand. So when I tell you that a teeny, tiny bag of gluten free oatmeal was $15.00 can you maybe understand why I am such a maniac about not using it for just anything?

What if something special occurs and I need it and I used the last flake of oat (Do oats come in flakes? What are they? Not kernels…) and I don't want to spend that much again on a container that is pretty much equal in size to a roll of dental floss!

I throw away my trash. I clean out my leftovers in the refrigerator. I do not have 37 cats. I think I am just fine on my end of the hoarding spectrum. Some of you are relating right now (it's okay to admit it) and some of you are thinking *isn't that why we buy food in the first place? Just EAT the stinking OATMEAL Jen Tucker!!!*

DING DONG!!

Literally saved by the doorbell from my organizational food paradox.

I walked to the door and saw that it was our insurance adjustor. This was the second time that he had been out to our house to take a peek at the damage and repairs thus far. The first time he was out to see us we still had carpets flapping in the breeze of industrial fans trying to suck the moisture out in several rooms. He and our water restoration company dissected a wall, and then two walls, and then all of our family room walls finding hidden moisture. What was just perhaps a few patches and coats of paint in the beginning turned into new walls. I learned so much from him (I will not mention any names for fear you will realize he is just a teddy bear and his tough exterior will be blown to bits).

He showed me lines in the structure, and ceiling depth in comparison to the walls and paint lines. He taught me about building code that was mandatory when our home was built and what had changed over the years. I remember sitting with him at the dining table (we had furniture delivered the day of the storm) and he began discussing with me numbers and policy coverage and the in's and out's of yada yada and as you can imagine I zoned out.

I tried to stay with him, but he lost me. I don't speak construction lingo. We talked about the insurance coverage we had on our home and he shared with me that this was a monumental storm that was not designated a tornado. However, it was strong enough to be considered catastrophic.

We were not the only victims of the storm. He told me about seeing the wrath of these winds at other homes. Feet of muck in a newly finished basement. A chimney that had tumbled down the side of a home and after taking chunks from the structure. After detaching, that good old chimney decided to stroll on down the street and check out the neighborhood. That chimney belonged to our friends Flan and Kristin.

He seemed a bit curious that I was so concerned about these other homes, and even though I wanted to get my issues dry walled and painted, I just could not imagine our chimney walking off the job, or my entire basement as a mud spa. From the beginning of this crazy event I always felt that we were spared and blessed because it could have been so much worse. Hearing first hand that it was much worse for others just made me even sadder for them.

We talked about the repair figures and he gave me an estimate for the work that he thought the cost should be that didn't quite match up with the contractor's but I know that is always part of it. Remember I told you about my friend Jocelyn? The one who had earlier expressed her utter stunned shock at the news of Gracie's arrival? She owns a fire, water, wind damage Construction Company with her husband Mike, so I know this is all just part of the way it goes. It's kind of a game really. The contractor charges for a nail and the labor to install that nail into the drywall, but the insurance company has the responsibility to do it in the most cost effective manner possible and as a result might even say something like they will pay for the nail, but not the labor cost to install said nail. Then, the contractor asks who will then be hitting the hammer to install the nail into the drywall to fix the damage to get the homeowner back in business since the insurance company is asking it to be done for free. Round and round we go.

I thanked our adjustor profusely for being so patient with me and explaining things to me so that I would really understand and feel competent enough to then explain it to Mike later. He stopped calculating and figuring and said, "You are about the nicest person I have ever been on a claim for. Why are you so nice?"

Huh? That's a weird question! I just kind of stopped and look at him thinking this could not be true that he found me nice and for it to be out of the ordinary.

I did not think too long before saying,"Why am I so nice? It takes to much energy to be mean. I don't have time for that!"

Why would you be mean to someone who is trying to help you and restore your home? Why wouldn't you listen and ask questions?

Recall the bank and TSA stories? Would you also place the insurance adjustor in that category as well of people to be courteous too? Honestly do you know how much energy it zaps from you to be crabby and in a bad mood and then take that out on others and ruin their mojo? What if I was the opposite? Had I been downright mean and rude to him and his next stop was your house, would you really want him there after I had irritated the snot out of him? I think not.

He also remarked that he could not believe how honest I was when seeing a crack in the lower level vinyl flooring that ran through a back hallway had damage as well, telling him that it was there prior to the storm. I have had this discussion many times and here is my take on honesty (and I am not going to fall back on that *it's the best policy* line).

Lying takes memory and mine is fading. If you tell one lie, it usually rolls into another. Then there is the effort to keep your story straight and remember who knows what and what was said to whom. You have to have a notion of why this falsehood started in the first place and that takes a lot of energy that I do not have. Not to mention the anxiety of being exposed as lying, or the being called out as the liar to the lie-ee. Plus the clincher is God is not a big fan of it, so I just don't do it! Why put that much work into crafting untruth? It will suck you dry!

Civility is a choice for many. To me it is not an option, it is a lifestyle, and as I try—and sometimes fail–as a parent the one thing I will not tolerate is a lack of kindness, courtesy, compassion, or humanity from my children. I may not have 19 kids, and can see how that might form a crazy line when you need a bathroom quickly. However the one thing that I have adopted that I heard Michelle Duggar teach her children was the J.O.Y. rule:

Jesus first

Others second

Yourself last

Isn't that simple? Yet we do not seem to be able to behave that way or embrace being other-centered for some reason. We forget that in our time of need when four inches of water is seeping up through our carpet, and the sunroom ceiling is bubbling and teetering on bursting with water to just be kind to others. Maybe our panties are in a bunch about something. That something isn't the end of the world is it?

I thanked him for his time and gave him a hug. Yes, I hugged my insurance adjustor! It turns out that my company was so overwhelming to him that he shared his experience with a friend. And as we exist in a world that has us all six degrees of separation from each other, it comes to pass that this man has a close relationship with a dear woman I know professionally. She has been there for me in sticky graduate school situations. Imagine if I had lied or was rude and he shared that with her. It would have questioned my character in a professional world where it is critical.

More than that, I would have been embarrassed that perhaps I missed my moment to shine a little love on another person. So live above the stuff that life throws your way.

Here's what I have learned about dealing with storm damage. If you get hung up on a little bit wet carpet being the end of your world, then you will miss the reason you are in this moment in the first place. Find J.O.Y and spread it around.

Breakfast at Tiffany's

So I embellish a bit…it's really lunch at Camille's and not so much the other place. If we had a Tiffany's in West Lafayette, first of all that would be a miracle of bizarre, parallel universe proportions. I would drool outside their store window every morning as Holly Golightly did and might need an intervention. I do not have any pieces of jewelry from there, but have given some glass pieces as wedding gifts over the years. I am hoping that in Nancy's last will and testament that she is leaving me her jewelry from the famous robin egg blue box store. She has some really cool pieces from there and I better start dropping hints and sucking up.

I was on my way to Camille's and while driving I passed my doctor's office and was suddenly struck with panic. It had slipped my mind all summer until this moment. I work with kids. I needed to get a TB test this summer and turn it into our building nurse the first week back to school. School starts Friday and my calendar said it was Wednesday. Oy vey! I grabbed my cell phone and called the office and made an appointment for after lunch. I am not horrified of needles but I am not a huge fan either.

I parked in the strip mall, but chose a spot close to the dry cleaner so I could trade some clothes with them. The dirty ones I had for the clean ones they'd already done. Mike was going to be leaving for a site visit in the states as soon as he returned and his only other suit was on his body in Germany, so I needed to make sure that *this* suit was cleaned, pressed and in the closet when he returned.

I seem to have this interesting issue when it comes to the cleaners. I forget to pick stuff up and I forget to drop stuff off. You might say that is a common problem for many of us but in my case I forget to drop stuff off when it is in the passenger's seat of my van sitting right next to me! It's like ignoring your shotgun driver, and it really is a problem. So to keep that from happening I placed the items needing a good scrub in a shopping bag and put them in the van next to my purse and cell phone so I would not forget to drop them off.

I walked around the corner and saw Cara standing in front of the restaurant. She was waiting for me and we gave each other a big hug. It was her birthday, an anniversary of her 21st birthday, and also our summer vacation was dwindling to a close. With all the hullabaloo concerning our house, and her daughter's being involved in summer travel sports, this was the first time we had seen each other all summer.

We texted all the time, but this was actual, real live human contact with my buddy. I just love this girl and I have the utmost respect for her. She is super cool and I can only aspire to be as cool as Cara is.

She works in the same school corporation as I do, and we share some of the same schools on our roster when it comes to working with kids. I have only known Cara since the beginning of January, but I feel like we are connected souls. It is a wonderful thing to have that type of rhythm with a colleague. I learn so much from her. We dine in her office during the school year and talk and about student progress and what we can do to help move them along developmentally and enhance their learning. We are total teacher geeks.

We do have a break in teacher talk to share stories about our children, husbands and our fascination with the Real Housewives franchise on Bravo. Our texts fly wild back and forth on new episode nights. It is total trash television, and watching it makes us feel so much better about our own self-worth in this life.

It is similar to the reason I used to watch Super Nanny with Mike. It made us feel so much better as parents just trying to survive the ropes of raising children by seeing the dysfunction of others. I am not proud to say it, but it is the truth.

Cara and I also bond over chocolate. There is no wrong time for it. It works in times of crisis to soothe the soul, it works to finish filling the stomach after lunch with just a little to top off the tank, it passes the time during webinars in her office and also trainings we attend.

Cara and I are passionate about many a chocolate. Chocolate on its own. Chocolate filled with peanut butter or caramel centers. Chocolate that has been married with nuts or nougat is bliss. Chocolate that envelops and ever so gently; lovingly surrounds a sweet bing cherry that once its center is pierced by a bite the rose` colored filling seeps out. Chocolate drizzled over fruit or twisted within a limb of a pretzel is pure paradise.

What is it about that salty and sweet combination of flavor that keeps us clamoring for more and we find ourselves not in the slightest satisfied with just a nibble? We must chow to the point of overdose. Semi sweet. Dark. Milk. All are welcome; however, never is white chocolate accepted into this fellowship of the sweets.

Well, there is one wrinkle in my denial of white chocolate taking membership in the league of chocolates. There is a candy made by Godiva I like. The little starfish white chocolates filled with raspberry.

My friend Teresa introduced me to them and I quickly and hastily dismissed them as faux sweets. I was shocked and appalled that any friend of mine would actually offer or advise me in regards to any type of white chocolate. I mean "non-chocolate" chocolate.

She taught me if you bite each point off of the star, then pop the rest of the treat into your mouth you will find the epicenter. The ratio of white chocolate to raspberry in this final act is forgivable. Why? You simply taste the raspberry; no white chocolate!   This vessel is simply the host to a filling waiting to burst onto the scene.

I tell you it could and should be replaced by any and all above said qualified chocolates. It's not the fillings fault that it was put here and so I have lifted my judgment of white chocolate on this solitary item and I truly mean only this item. White chocolate peanut butter cups? Laughable! White chocolate Easter bunnies? Deplorable! Don't get me started on carob…

Cara and I ordered our salads and carried them over to a comfy granny smith apple green booth and began to chow down. She shared with me her travelling softball summer stories, and I caught her up to speed on my morning that had already started off with a butter fugitive on the run being hunted by half naked detectives in pink polka dotted boots. She was mulling over how to spend her birthday evening and was so happy to spend part of it to me.

Cara has a husband who travels a great deal during the week and has also come to embrace the term married single parent to describe many of the days on their calendar. She understands what it is like to run the house solo, but could not relate to the runaway dog issues. I keep telling Cara her girls need a dog. She would rather get them a Bob the frog that would sit on her kitchen counter in a small plastic cube. That way he could live his life not really interfering with hers.

As all good things come to an end, summer is one of them and ours flew by at warp speed.

"Happy Birthday my birthday girl!"

"Thanks Tuck. I'm glad I got to spend it having lunch with you."

100

We had a great time catching up and before I had realized it a few moments became hours. I gave her a hug and we walked out together towards our cars.

"Jen, where's your van?"

"Oh, I parked it around the corner. I wanted to park in front of the dry cleaners so I wouldn't forget to drop off Mike's stuff.

Cara grinned. Shook her head.

"What is going on with you and that dry cleaner? Are you seeing him on the side? I've never seen anyone at the cleaners as much as you J. Tuck!"

"That's because no one forgets to take their stuff to the cleaners as often as me!"

We laughed. We hugged.

"Did you at least put your clothes into your car this time or are they sitting in your driveway again?"

"No smarty-pants, I put them in a bag and placed them right behind my seat so I would not forget them."

Cara was referring to the time I realized that my dry cleaning was missing! At the time I was teaching school and working on my Master's Degree.

I was convinced someone stole all my clothes out of my car! I was freaking out because I had a few pairs of pants in there, but Mike's suit was gone. Gone-gone!

Oh good Lord was I in a state.

I drove home sweating, hoping upon hope that I had left them on the bench that graces the wall near the front door. When I pulled into the driveway there sat the bag of cleaning smack dab in the middle of it. It had been sitting out all day. My feelings finding this bag in the driveway were mixed. A dab of relief, folded in gently with worry that some furry creature might be roosting in there now.

The worst part was that I knew by the time on my watch that my oldest son, Wil, was already home. Ryan was a 5th grader at the time and also had returned from school. That means they both had walked up the driveway and walked on by the bag. After a quick peek inside it, checking for non-rent paying rodents, I picked up the bag and walked into the house. I held up the bag in front of both boys as they sat at the kitchen table.

"Did you guys see this bag in the driveway?
They both shook their heads yes not looking up from afterschool snacks to grace me even with a glance.

"Why on earth would you leave a sack of clothes in the middle of the driveway and just walk on by it?"

Ryan looked at me and said, "Why would *you* leave it in the driveway?"

"It was an accident Ryan, it wasn't on purpose," I said in a sarcastic tone that seemed to mirror the one he uses from time to time.

"Huh! I thought you left those out for someone to have like you cleaned out your closet or something."

Wil still had his head buried in a bowl of potato chips.

"Is that because I normally leave a bag of clothes in the middle of the driveway for some random person to take Ryan? Because that *is* what I do every day."

"You do that every day Mom?" Ryan said in all seriousness.

He didn't get it. My sarcasm was laid on a little too thick and I retreated to my neutral corner. Mothers of preteens often call that our own personal time-out. Either we put ourselves in timeout voluntarily or the storms clouds roll in and we can roll to the dark side very quickly.

But I was not in that memory. I was safely with Cara laughing about dry cleaning stories and preparing to remember to drop off and pick up our clothes.

I gave Cara another hug and slipped around to corner to my car. As I walked towards it, I unlocked the doors with my key fob then hit the button to open the sliding door behind the driver's side. As the door slid open, the sack of dry cleaning that I thought I had put there was not there. I poked my head in and looked towards the passenger's side thinking I placed it there. Nada. Well shoot, I must have put it in the trunk and so I walked around to the back of my van, opened it up and there in all its glory was a lonely receipt for water softener salt and a dog leash. Is there a conspiracy against me today? No bag of dry cleaning. Yes, I know; check my driveway when I get home.

536 Pounds Ma'am

After leaving Cara and not going to the cleaners, I realized that I had time to run to the hardware store around the corner and get some type of contraption for my dogs to have in the yard. I had stopped by Wal-Mart before meeting Cara and they had a few dog runs, but nothing that I saw looked like it had the wherewithal to sustain gale force winds and pressure of the canine order. In our house we use a couple of different terms for this store—well, obviously we use its actual name. We affectionately call it Wally World. My friend Dana coined it The Evil Empire – you try to escape and go to Target but due to its proximity it sucks you in and you cannot escape its tractor beam.

Give me a small helpful hardware folk over a big box store any day. Don't get me wrong the big guys have their place and I appreciate being able to go look at aisles upon aisles of new toilet seats. There is something about the personal service and feel of your neighborhood store that can never be found in those massive rows upon rows.

Maybe it is because for so long we had our own family business that being a patron to one is important to me. Regardless, I was on a mission and needed a chain or cable or something STAT! Did I sound like George Clooney in E.R.? Here goes my sidebar on George.

I love him! The dashingly handsome smile, the whit and swagger. Those eyes that convey to me that the mischief in his soul just might match the quantity in mine. It's all delicious and delectable. I know he is on someone's list of men that makes their heart pitter pat. I have had conversations with my girlfriends about "The List of Three."

Maybe you have such a list. It's the one where if you ever cross paths with someone that you deem dreamy and a "must have" then this person's name is tattooed on your list of people you would want to have a romantic encounter with. No holds barred and game on kind of thing. I know couples where husband and wife have a list such as this, and they love to compare notes and laugh about the idea of an indecent proposal with the ones that they conjure up images of steamy incidentals with.

Now I know you are wondering if I have a list. I do have one, but my "List of Three" is quite different. It is not full of unobtainable conquests that I want to be with intimately in a physical sense. I personally feel that is disrespectful to my husband and soul mate. He is my world and the only man for me in every area of my life. My list contains people that I think would make me laugh so hard I would pee through a Depends undergarment.

They would challenge me and engage me in great conversation as we sit belly up at an open air bar for hours. They would love a good drink on the rocks whether it is hard liquor or tonic water with a lime. My list does include George Clooney. The legendary prankster and humanitarian, who acts from time-to-time. He would catch me up to speed on his humanitarian efforts, in between recalling practical jokes on Brad Pitt and what he did to torture the bus driver as an elementary student.

He would sit in a simple t-shirt and cargo shorts with mirrored shades shaking the ice cubes in his glass to swirl and clink as I laugh and toss back my tendrils. I am not shaking my hair from my face to be sexy; rather it is stuck to my lip gloss and tastes nasty from all the hairspray. Mike is actually with us, but as we sit at the bar and I face my BFF Cloon Dog, my beloved sits behind me or on the other side of our friend so my view will not be blocked of his royal cuteness.

We would talk about Tootie and Blair Warner and what the "facts of life" really are all about. Before we really hit the tequila shooters he would casually mention to me that his bike was parked around the corner and would ask me to take a ride with him through the hills of L.A. I would have to do a 180 degree spin to meet Mike's eyes to get an idea of his thoughts on the matter. He in turn would be pushing my rear off the barstool to get moving so that he can have a turn when we are finished.

When we return from our hour long ride and I nurse the red marks on my cheeks where bugs flew into me at speeds of up to 100 miles an hour, Mike would have his turn taking a spin. They would only ride around the block because what could they possibly want to see in the scenery if I am not there? Seriously!

Back at Wal-Mart. They had nada. I was back in my van and heading to a little hardware store down the street.

I was only a few steps into the store before someone in a red vest stopped me and asked me if I needed any help finding things. Such a helpful hardware dude! Can I just say when you go into a store and someone asks if they can help and you know what you want to find, why don't you tell them?

Saying you are "Just looking" is fine if you are truly doing so, but if you know what you want and are offered help just say yes! Do you know how much time you will save in your life if you let a more knowledgeable person help you? Do you know that the person who helps you feels really good about themselves when they can lend a hand? So, I explained what I was looking for and the gentleman passed me on to someone named Mark.

I explained my massively large dog situation and that I needed a run line, or long chain; something to keep Jack and Henry in their yard and not out on walk-abouts in my hood. Mark stooped down over the bottom shelf and then popped back up with a package. Included was a contraption that you placed between two trees in your yard and the cable would stretch between them with a balancing pulley thing that connected to a long leash (I was not an engineering major). In theory, the dog could run between the trees on this long leash and move about the yard.

The theory left out the fact that my dogs have the superhero power of being Houdini's and I worried they would be able to escape. You should have seen the width of this cable. I want you to imagine a spaghetti noodle that is uncooked. Now picture a thin spaghetti noodle uncooked. Now picture sewing floss that you use to cross-stitch with. Not the entire unrolled floss, but the individual strands that you separate before threading you needle. Somewhere in there you have the circumference of this cable that was marketed and created to keep my 100 pound a piece dogs from breaking free. I think not.

I asked Mark if there was another solution that we could come up with. Like taking a thick linked chain and attaching a fastener at one end where I would clip it to the dog's collar, and securing it on the other end to a stake that goes into the ground. Maybe making the chain 10 feet long so the boys could each have a nice round about in the yard, yet put them close enough that they could interact but not get tangled up. It worked for our Lhasa Apso we had when I was younger and he weighed 20 pounds soaking wet. I thought that I had a brilliant plan.

I asked Mark's opinion on which type of chain would work best. I didn't want it to poke or rub the dog's fur wrong or cause injury and some of them looked as if they came straight off the barbarian battlefields. Ouchie! He showed me a chain that was super thick, smooth all around the edges and said that it would withstand "536 pounds of pressure Ma'am." That sounded good. Then we looked at the connector brackets that would anchor to the triangle shaped stake-thing that would spin into the earth and stake it into the ground. Again, not an engineer. Mark told me that the stakes were guaranteed to hold up to 300 pounds of pressure. Wow! We are now talking about almost 850 pounds of combined force that would stand up to each dog respectively. At least that was the math equation in my head! I'm in! SOLD!

I was not always so confident in a home improvement store. There was a time where I didn't even walk in one solo. That stuff was always on Mike's *Honey You Do It* lists. No thank you! Metal things and bolts that connect to thingamabobs, and then you have the aisle of splinters aplenty were all those planks of wood waited to attack me. And who knew that there were so many different paints? Not just types like oil or latex, but the shelves upon shelves of spray paint and wood stains! PANIC ATTACK!

One day my little world opened and welcomed in a little something called HGTV. Are you with me now? This little miracle gave me exposure to how to be a fix it gal around the house and make it a prettier place to be and not be afraid to do it yourself. Do not misunderstand me, if Candice Olson or Jeff Lewis showed up on my doorstep and begged me to let them remodel my home I would throw open the doors and enthusiastically invite them inside. I believe that empowerment is fundamental to taking action.

Thank you Jeff Lewis for not letting me fear painting my kitchen two shades of green! Thank you Steve Thomas for telling me that I cannot mess up a chargeable screwdriver and to Nate Berkus, for convincing me that if I actually used a level to hang mirrors, paintings and whatnots that it would keep me from whipping hammers at windows like a frustrated golfer on the green.

Mark counted out two sets of chain each ten feet long, helped me gather the other items I needed and I headed to the counter to pay for my goodies. Have you ever carried 20 feet of chain link and all the goodies that accompany it? HEAVY!!!! I got into the van and let the bag fall to the floor. The van echoed with every clunk and clink imaginable as I fumbled with my keys to start the engine. Ha! No one with four legs is leaving my yard now!!!

Wiggling Needles

"Chain, chain, chaaaaaaaaaaain! Chain my doooooogs!"

I was belting out my own lyrics to the melody of the song Chain of Fools and feeling those high notes! I have little, to no shame. Don't you just wish you were in the car next to me while I drove to the doctor? My next stop; TB test!

I have no fear of needles. Bring it! I do not mind inoculations or skin test that requires the injection of a vial's contents to bubble under the skin. This TB test is no biggie! You can take a gallon of blood from my arm and I will watch without fear of vomit, fainting or glass shattering screams of drama. It does not gross me out and I really find it fascinating to watch the red flow into the collection tube.

That is liquid life people!

What pumps through our hearts and veins keeps us alive. I am really tough as long as you do not prick my finger. If you prick my finger I will not be your friend anymore. We are through--done. The first time I remember the finger prick, which I like to think of as a steel rod piercing my dainty flesh, being an issue for me is when Mike and I were getting insurance policies as young marrieds.

There was a nurse who came to our small apartment and she needed to collect blood to make sure that we were healthy as horses. I remember her telling us that she would need a blood sample and I immediately began rolling up my sleeve. She smiled at me and told me that would not be necessary because she was going to prick my finger.

I remember wishing I had some type of horrible injury that I could pick a scab! I know I just made you cringe and I wish I could apologize for it but I cannot do it, because I am totally serious! Just the thought of a finger prick and my hands go clammy. My fingers go numb and then cold. I try to breathe and think of other mind relieving things but I am telling you, I think that is bologna! It hurts, I hate it; don't want to do it! Then when I see that contraption come near me where the nurse pushes this button over the tip of your finger and you hear this click that echoes throughout the room, I lose my mind.

The anticipation of that noise is too much for me to bear. My breathing quickens and I can feel my pulse beat in my head. I am getting a little freaked out just typing about it! It's like being attacked by a mega, giga, strata-sized thumbtack!

Here is the worst part of the whole situation. I am so upset, and so out of sorts that when my torturer pops that button (it might as well be the sound of a lowering guillotine blade) to draw blood from my finger, I am a zero collection. No blood. My only theory is that when my ears here that I am going to have to go through this extraction of my life force, my eyes seeing this encroaching hooligan moving towards me that my brain must yell "RETREAT" to every drop of blood in my hands and orders it to pool in any and every other available foxhole in my body.

If you think about it this explanation is quite logical. It accounts for the clammy and pale digits that go numb. Yes, they pinch and squeeze the snot out of the tip of my finger to attempt to juice just a drop of blood, but I am a dry well. If you think that means I am off the hook, you are sadly mistaken. If you think that I beat the system, you are wrong. That just means that they move in for the kill on another finger. And this time, there is no countdown to impact. There is usually the niceties that they will be gentle, and sorry we must repeat this who thing but then they grab my finger and skewer the crud out of me! You know, you never really realize how deep your trauma issues run until you recall them play by play.

So I have to come clean. I need to tell you that there was a time I went from the belief that a blood draw from the crook of my arm being no big deal, to becoming a huge exploitation of my inalienable rights. When I was pregnant with Wil I flunked the gestational diabetes test we all love taking so much. There was no breakfast for me that morning. I went into my doctor's office for the blood draw and received a failing grade. This meant that I needed to come back a few days later, camp out at the lab for three hours and experience a blood test once called the 3 hr GTT. First, your blood is taken to have a baseline. After drinking a super sweet, nasty orange beverage, they draw blood from you once an hour, for three hours. The beverage was served to me in a little glass bottle that looked like a tiny bottle of flavored seltzer water. If only it tasted as good.

I remember when seltzers busted onto my scene when I was about 10 years old. My mom bought every flavor that we could get our hands on at the local grocer. The brand that we were hooked on was called New York Seltzers and my favorite concoction was to mix the vanilla flavor beverage with the raspberry. You just do not understand how magical that was in my mouth. Trust me, this citrusy, sugary junk tastes nothing like that, and there was no magic.

Mike dropped me off for my appointment for that morning. When you are pregnant and go without eating, with the exception of drinking disgusting amounts of glucose to rev up your engine for a blood sample once an hour for three hours, there is a slight fear of fainting. So although no one warned me to have a famine free driver, in my "Jen brain" it made sense not to pass out at the wheel. The love of my life, Mr. Mike Tucker, was my chauffer that morning. After pulling up to the front door of the medical building, I gave Mike a kiss and made my exit from the car. Not so daintily, I waddled into the building and then into the elevator. I found the chair closest to the bathroom in my doctor's office, plopped into a chair and set up shop. Just me, my belly and a good book.

I have no recollection of what the book was. Could have been the top million baby names ever sired, tips on how not to commit husband homicide when hormonal, the best seller of 1996. I have no idea so regardless if it was good or not, I blame pregnant brain for blocking it out of my memory.

"Jennifer?" I heard a voice call with that lilt at the end that was looking for me. My eyes met this sweet, little old lady who reminded me of my grandma June. She had little rimmed glasses, and rosy pink stained lips. Her white hair was set in short curls and looked as if she rolled each one of them before she slept each night. She was a little thing; thin and short in stature. I smiled and wiggled up off my chair.

I followed her back to the sterile room thinking I had the most comforting escort ever. She asked me about the baby and how I was feeling which I am sure she asked several times a day to several women at different stages in this journey of impending motherhood. Yet it felt like that question was only meant for me and I savored it.

She opened the mini refrigerator and pointed to several bottles of beverages I could choose from to drink for this test. I grabbed the orange flavor. It looked least threatening. She showed me back out to the waiting room and gave me strict instructions to drink it quickly and then she would be back in an hour to take me back to draw my blood. She patted my leg and left me with this task to swig it down like a champ, and I did just that. It was tough to do, and tasted so syrupy, yet I conquered it. That was simple enough. I can do that a few more time! No problem...

Time ticked off the clock and before I knew it, my sweet little granny friend came for me and escorted me back to the phlebotomist. She kept looking over her shoulder to make sure I was behind her and I was hanging in there. We came into the

114

little white room full of vials, and spinning things with samples inside. I saw several digital timers, neat patient files and lots and lots of gauze and band aids.

She seated me in a chair and asked me which arm worked best for a blood draw. *Huh?! Aren't you just my sweet granny escort back here so I will not be nervous?* I suddenly became a selective mute and pointed to my right arm while not taking my eyes off of her.

Oh I get it!

Oh! I get it! She preps the patients for the lab and any minute the *real* person drawing my blood will pop in!

I convinced myself that the lab staff must be on a snack break or emergency Band-Aid run. That's it; they were out of neon pink quick-fixes to keep pressure taught against that big wad of cotton they stuff in the crook of your arm. They were moments away. They'd be back any minute. And as I negotiated this conversation in my head, she was wrapping rubber tubing around my right bicep. Our eyes met and she smiled at me. It was at this moment that her little rimmed glasses held the most substantial magnification of eyeballs in a lens I had ever seen! Her eyeballs were blown up to the size of pool balls! I think that my notice of her massive vision assistance caught her *eye*.

"Oh honey, are you a little nervous? Don't you worry because I have been doing this long before your Momma swallowed a watermelon!"

WHAT THE HECK DOES MY MOM'S DIGESTIVE HABITS HAVE TO DO WITH THIS!!!!

What she was saying to me in a terribly conveyed fashion was that she had been doing this long before my mom was pregnant with me. That was of zero satisfaction to me at this moment. My God, how many Jen's did she see in those glasses?

117

And the fact that you seem to have tried to comfort me with the fact you have been doing this since the Stone Age made me want to run. I didn't run.

I sat there and calmed myself down. Maybe I should calm down in general, and not be so judgmental! I mean if she was doing this professionally, there had to be someone, somewhere who made sure she was able to perform her duties to the best of her vampire abilities right? So then I felt bad. I judged her abilities and there was definitely some ageism in there and I was not proud of that. I realigned my circumstantial evidence pertaining to this situation. I wiped the fright off my face and replaced it with a smile. It might have been a fantastic and plastic smile, but a smile it was.

I watched her prep the vial into the needle and grab all the necessities to carry out this transaction. Nothing seemed to cause alarm yet, so maybe I was all worked up for nothing. She began tapping on my veins. Looking for the plumpest one of the bunch. She told me I would feel a "little stick." That I was prepared for. Like I said, I can give blood all day out of my arm. No big deal. But that is when it happened.

The needle went in with no problem, but once in my arm I could feel it wiggle. It moved back and forth. Not just a slight jarring. Not a onetime shimmy, but a constant back and forth, back and forth, back and forth. I bit my tongue. I chomped on my lip. There was no way I was going to make a big scene while that needle was still inside there due to the fear of something worse happening in my screech of pain. What if I scared this granny vampire literally to death? Could I have been charged with manslaughter if that happened? Those thoughts were swirling between my ears. Thankfully, as I was lost in my own little world of birthing my baby in prison, she pulled the needle out and plopped the gauze on top of the puncture. She bent my arm for me to wedge the cotton in place and stop the bleeding. Thank you God that was over!

Granny Vampire walked me back out front, gave me another bottle of a confectionary woe to swig down and left me back in my chair. I was *stuck* here, pun intended, at least for another hour until she returned for the next extraction and maybe this time she would suck my soul out too! She was a wolf in sheep's clothing. She was a blood-thirsty creature. Where was *my* granny when I needed her to beat the crud out of this lady?

I prayed the next 3600 seconds would tick off the clock as slowly as possible. I prayed that she was first shift and the pterodactyl time clock she might have been used too was going to sound any moment. Then she would go home in her Flintstone mobile. Quite the opposite occurred and I found myself right back that chair with her tapping my left arm this time. I couldn't stay silent.

"Last time you drew my blood it was a little painful."

"Oh I'm so sorry dear. I truly am. I promise I will be a little gentler this time."

How to tread lightly with someone hovering over me with a finely honed object? With intent to stab.

"You know, it wasn't so much being gentle last time you drew my blood. It was just painful in my vein."

"Oh dear me, I am so, so sorry! Maybe you have sensitive veins. So many mommies-to-be do. How about I use a smaller needle this time? One they use for children? And maybe that right arm of yours feels a little more sensitive than your left sweetie so we will use that arm this time."

Well heck yeah lady! Bust that one out if it is going to be easier for you to manage and not cause me to want to become unglued! And you know, maybe she was right. Perhaps I had a little abnormal sensitivity in my arm right now. Hormones are sensitive. My boobs are sensitive. It makes sense right? Maybe the mambo I felt in my arm earlier was not even her fault.

So she inserted the smaller needle. The smaller the needle, the worse the wiggle! I swore she worked covert as a hit man on the side. What a great cover she had going. You think this sweet granny is going to make you cookies and rub Vick's Vapo Rub on your chest when you're sick, but that is so not the case. Granny Vampire is literally out for my blood! If my Grandma was here at this moment she would be going back-hills Kentucky all over her! Miss Eddie Lee McCoy of the feuding Hatfield and McCoys. I know what I am talking about. It's more than protective Grandmotherly instinct!

Another orange bottle of gunk. Me in the waiting room. Shaking from sugar overload, being a pin cushion twice over, and a starving baby momma. I am sure that I was a theater district sign. In neon lights you could see that I was the perfect hodgepodge of shambles. I will never cease to be amazed that our Heavenly Father knows just what we need when we need it. At that moment I needed support and in walked my husband. Mike said he didn't want me to be alone for the last test. When I caught sight of him I began to weep. I tried to hold it back but the flood gates opened as I buried my head in his shoulder attempting through the sobs and hot mess I had become to tell him in a hushed voice what had painfully transpired. He grabbed my face in his hands; wiped away my tears. When I looked at his forehead it was all wrinkled. His pupils dilated. Sperm donor was not happy someone used his baby momma as cross-stitch fabric.

"I'm gonna say *something* to *somebody* and I am gonna say it *right now*!"

"No you are not saying anything! You aren't! You promise me!"

"Baby, you sit here and tell me that this old lady stuck you so badly that it hurt. You tell me these things while you are crying! I am talking to someone."

"You are gonna make it *ten times* worse for me! Promise me you won't say anything! You swear it. Mike… *Mike!*"

He didn't promise. He didn't say anything! He didn't have time.

"Jennifer can you come with me please?"

I looked up and the voice was different, the body was different, and I realized it was a young brunette thing that called out to me and not Granny Vampire! You have no idea for a gal sugared out of her gourd and starving how quickly I perked up. From being at almost Def-Con 4 on the fainting scale, I popped up and whipped my sleeve up for the blood-letting to commence!

This was my new best friend. Her name irrelevant. She saved me and I was eternally grateful. Is it wrong to love someone so deeply that you just met? Someone you just said had an irrelevant name? I walked back for the third and last time to the little, white sterile room. I was about to give my blood for the greater good of my womb, this sweet angel from heaven introduced herself.

"Jennifer, my name is _____. I am a medical student studying phlebotomy. Would it be okay if I drew your blood for this last test?"

She smiled eagerly. I stared at her student ID. Rather than ask to see her resume of total blood draws to date, median number of misses and tendon hits, I frowned.

And with a whimper asked, "Is Granny Vampire available?"

Burning Layers

Did you really think in these days where zombie apocalypses and vampires steal the media scene I wouldn't include one? Well it's the last fanged character you will find here. While we are on the subject, let me tell you something about Vampires. They do not glitter. Vampires should burn to a crisp in daylight. That is how it has always been and forever shall be! And they have fangs! Vicious, blood-thirsty fangs! Please don't hate me. I am a vampire purist. I love them just the way they are.

I left the doctor's office with my TB test over and it was flawlessly completed. No inappropriate use of needles! In my wisdom I now possess in these prime years of life, I quickly share my Vampire Granny experience with everyone who enters my sphere of living that wants to have their way with me in a medical sense. I pass it off as a joke, but in all seriousness I want it known that I expect a 30 second professional commercial explaining why they are the most qualified in the building to perform their task. Again, it is not the needle I fear. It is the wiggle.

I walked in my front door and found my boys just freshly off the bus from school. Thank God I missed the actual dropping off and walking up the driveway part. Heaven forbid a repeat of yesterday's parental mishap. I am met with love, affection, the blissful information that no one has homework to finish. After they check out my newly minted lump on my arm, the question of the day hits. Ryan volunteers to ask it.

"What's for dinner?"

This is a little late in the day actually for it to occur. It usually happens over breakfast before my kids leave for a day of learning. The question my children ask me habitually is what we are going to eat for dinner. My friends who also have teenage boys say they have the same conversations with their sons. Not really their daughters mind you, but those raging testosterone bodies of boys must be fed. In their minds they must know and file away the information of what will be deposited into their stomachs later in the day.

The problem with this question is that it is multilayered. You must read between the lines because there is a lot more going on here than meets the eye. My sons want to know many things with this question.

Is it something palatable?

What is the accompanying vittles and do they have some type of condiment for dipping because that would horrify them.

Is there some type of reward other than the good feeling and full belly that you have for cleaning your plate? Such as a 12 layer cake. Are they are delusional? Do they think that I made said cake, and have stashed it in some top secret vault somewhere? Yes, I made a 12 layer cake in all my Julia Child spare time during the day.

The nitty-gritty is that they are trying to get to is this point. Are we having what our household calls, "Wish Sandwiches." What are those pray tell? Wish Sandwiches is defined in the Tucker family dictionary as the time when you have two pieces of bread and *wish* that you had something to put between them. When we say it's Wish Sandwich night, it means if you can make it and it is somewhat nutritionally sound, by all means you go right ahead and make it. Cereal? Great! Grilled cheese? You go crazy! If you can bake it, broil it or sauté it then you go ahead and get crafty in the kitchen.

We have a lot of Wish Sandwich nights when Mike is gone. For my kids it is the "TV Dinner" of my generation. My father would travel for work between the states and Europe before he became a professor in the early 1980's and believe you me, my mom would stock up on those babies! I never wanted the ones with that nasty vanilla pudding in the middle. I chose my dinner based on the dessert that was offered. My favorite TV dinner dessert was the crispy apple cobbler that baked up to a nice golden bubbly. It makes my mouth water just thinking about it, but those little dishes of yum came to a crashing halt in my life.

Most men when they hit their midlife crisis get a fast car, a girlfriend, a sleeve of tattoos and the likes. Not my father. He quits his high paying engineering job in the burbs of Connecticut, moves my mom and I from our quiet cul-de-sac home situated on over two acres of scenic views to Toledo, Ohio. He became a professor making less than poverty level salary, and we lived in a two bedroom townhouse with a track full of trains that rumbled behind us at all hours of the day and night.

Despite how bad it sounds I want you to know something. It was God who led this change in my Dad's direction. It was his best friend Harold who gave him a spark at the possibility to mold young minds and make a different difference in this world. It was a church experience while passing through Toledo during the holidays with Harold and his wife Janice that led to my parents finding God in a real and revealing way.

Just when you think you are just popping by on your way from Michigan back to Connecticut over Christmas Break, your course changes in life. Today my father is at Purdue University celebrating his 22nd year on campus. He recently *stepped up* (as my dad coins it) into faculty from years at the helm of his department.

He is a sought after speaker. He contributes to several publications and is an author. All because he listened to that still small voice that said, "Move." I will have you know all of this is to say that this move to Ohio was the end of my Swanson's

Salisbury Steak TV dinner stretch because who had the money for such luxury now? My *Wish Sandwiches* truly became wish sandwiches.

My middle schoolers were relieved at the reminder that Margie was coming over tonight with her husband Jon and bringing us dinner. There are days that I tell Margie she should just quit her job as a college counselor and cook for me. Not for pay mind you, but because she loves me. She is a primo kitchen whiz and it is pure pleasure anytime I can sink my teeth into one of her cuisine concoctions. Margie was only allowed to bring us a meal if they would then stay and break gluten free bread with us. Not only do I love their company, but I needed all the extra adult companionship I could get for as long as I could retain it over the coming days.

My calendar reminder buzzed loudly on my phone and I realized Wil had an appointment that I needed to take him too. We headed towards our destination, he seated next to me in the front. I drive what I like to call my stretch Honda Accord with the open trunk feature, definitely not a minivan.

"How was your day?"

"It was great Mom!"

"Really? Do you like being an 8th grader now Wil?"

"I do because that means next year I go to high school and then four years later…no more school for me!"

"Wil, it warms my heart that you are so goal oriented," I say with just a hint of mommy mockery.

He laughed right back at me with the same depth of satire.

"Mom, did you know there are only 18 more days until Labor Day and that is our first vacation day off school? That is 12 school days with no weekends."

"Are you doing just as many calculations in your math class as you are with the school year calendar?"

"I figured it out on the bus this morning, not in math class Mom."

"Hey! I'm just glad you are doing math bud!"

Wil and I drove for a while and pulled into the parking lot outside of the building we were summoned too. The place and type of location we were at is not really necessary for me to share. **Reason one:** *I do not want to get sued!* **Reason two:** not knowing "the whom," the what, and where it is not going to keep you from understanding the gist of the story. It was not a tattoo parlor, nor was it a juvenile probation office, and please know that it was no house of ill-repute. I mean this person no harm and would like to keep it all neutral.

I began putting the car into park when my cell phone rang. It was my contractor wanting to know if there was any update from our insurance company. I covered the phone on my end and told Wil to go ahead on in and I would be right there. Wil hopped out of the car and walked towards the building. The contractor and I chatted for a while about the visit earlier that morning from the insurance company. I shared the fact that the main concern for the insurance company could be the estimate to fix the damage. Since the voice on the other line was so dear to me outside of the reconstruction world, our conversation shifted for a time just checking in on each other's day-to-day stuff and excused myself after a few moments to be with Wil.

I walked into the building, and found a chair. I was an ear shot away from Wil. Wil was speaking to this person about the evolution of the relationship between Sandy Cheeks and SpongeBob Squarepants. More than friends? Two creatures from different biospheres attempting to "make it work." I listened to Wil try to engage this person in conversation. I heard the response back to my son in a tone and demeanor that just caught my momma bear instincts to swell up within me. Don't mess with Momma Bear; definitely don't mess with her cubs. The curt brush off my son was enduring was difficult for me.

You might think I was overreacting. In hindsight I agree with you. But I couldn't squash the anger in my gut. I have been in this "sheltering" mode before when it comes to my children; especially with Wil. Always with Wil.

July 23, 1996 at 6:00am I was admitted into the hospital to give birth to my first child. It was the summer of the Olympics in Atlanta. The times I craved Olive Garden Breadsticks and Eli's cheesecake nonstop were about to end. My feet were at the breaking point of swelling. Ugh, did that ever happen to you? My toes, feet and ankles looked like Play-Doh! Press your fingers into my skin and the imprint would stay. The only shoes that fit? Mike's flip flops. It was definitely a "Glamour Don't" look just like in the back of the magazines. Guess what? I could have cared less!

My nurse was hooking me up to monitors and medicines that hung from poles when my doctor entered the room. Can I just tell you how much I adored my doctor? A second generation OB/GYN who handled hormonal freakshows like me with grace. At every appointment for the past two weeks, I begged him to induce me. It bordered tantrum really. He would smile and cheer me on. Then I would cry. He would tell me it was almost over. And as I pled my case, my doctor with his grayish hair and a shared love of my treasured Lake Michigan, became the soothsayer of the east. He did the Jedi mind trick on me somehow. I went from crazed woman ready to pop right there, to being easily convinced that I could hang on a little bit longer. I can only compare it to being able to raise the Titanic from its permanent address by using a shoestring to lift it. Impossible right?

But he was magic I tell you. Mike only wishes he had such powers. I constantly tell Mike, "Your powers are weak old man!"

A little rap on the door. "Good morning Jen how are you feeling?" he smiled.

You would think I was smiling too right? This was it! Game time! The moment I carried on about for weeks.

"I am feeling like you have 12 hours to get this baby out. Tomorrow is my third anniversary and I am not baking Mickey Mouse birthday cakes for the rest of my life on my anniversary." Pretty blunt wouldn't you say?

My doctor patted my leg all bundled in blankets. "We will do our best," he said with that same magical spell. It took me from high octane crabby thinking; *I am going to punch this dude*, to feeling like he was on "Team Jen." How did he do that?

Time ticked off the clock. Labor is not that bad when you chose drugs and you chose them early. Dare I say when you mix painkillers with Dum-Dum suckers and ice chips life is good! Why be a hero and go "natural" A.K.A. drug free? You can be woman and still roar not feeling a dang thing from the waist down you know.

In the wee hours we call 3:00AM I was ready to push. 19 hours after we were admitted. Okay so I had never done this pushing thing before. I couldn't feel a thing (YAY!). First baby mom's, you know what I mean!

The drill sergeant nurses gave me orders about the way this whole birth process was going to happen. Honestly at that point, I could've cared less if the baby was coming out my nostrils. I think I was flunking previously said military orders, because I got the spiel from them about "new moms can be here pushing a long time" and "the sooner we can get this baby out the better I would feel." Again, can you just pull it out my nostrils and we can be done here? And who is the 'we' in this situation? You might be an unlucky bystander in my current scenario. The drill sergeant. An active participant. I am the only one naked on the table in this room. You are not. Therefore we are not a "we."

As the hours of pushing went on, as I was assured this happens with so many first time labors, I just knew something was wrong. I didn't feel a change in pressure that I should have as Wil tried to make an exit. When we hit the three hour mark, the nurses called the doctor into the room. He discovered that Wil was transverse; sideways as if he had rolled over onto his right side and stayed there with no idea his little rollover did not help matters. His heart rate was dropping not during but between my contractions. This had become a bad situation far quicker than Mike and I could process.

My doctor sat next to me on the bed and calmly told me that he was going to scrub up and meet me in the operating room shortly. My nurses were running around the room getting me prepped as he was talking, and although he never let me hear the gravity of the situation, the chaos I saw around him told me what I needed to know. Nurses hiding panic with fake smiles is nothing you want to see.

My new surgical nurse stepped in and handed Mike scrubs. He popped into the bathroom and changed at what I can only describe as Superman phone booth quick-change speed. Mike kissed my cheek and forehead.

"I love you baby. I'm going to go talk to our parents."

He kissed my head again.

"You're going to be okay, you know?"

I nodded my head yes. He kissed me again. Mike left; the door slamming behind him.

The time was hovering around 6:00am at this point. An entire day had passed in residence at the hospital.

I found myself alone for just a moment. Everyone had stepped out of the room. I did not find terror or fear. I did not go to *what if's* or other should haves and could haves. I placed my hands on my belly and prayed through tears of love and compassion for my son.

There was no desperation in my plea, but one of healing and promises God's plans not to harm us, but prosper us. That he knows us while still in the womb and knows every hair that will grow on my sweet baby's head one day. And then I just rested in the silence of the moment.

At the same time I made my pleas, my soul mate had come around the corner in the waiting room wearing his scrubs. He saw our parents stop speaking mid-conversation intermixed with laughter and rise from their chairs. All four were anticipating Mike giving them the news they had been in suspension for during these past nine months. They saw the tears fall down Mike's face. He reached out to embrace his mom.

"I'm going to lose them. I'm going to lose both of them!" The pain in his voice was too immense for my parents and they embraced each other sobbing. Mike's parents did their best to help him regain some type of automatic pilot to make it through. My dad hugged Mike.

"Michael, they are going to be fine. We are all here for you. We love you. Go be with my little girl."

It was this moment as Mike spilled his fears of losing both Wil and I in a matter of minutes that somehow my Daddy, the man who taught me to spit off the top of the Eiffel Tower, calmed the monsters in my bedroom closet, held me close as I stepped upon the tops of his shoes to dance with him, my biggest cheerleader at all my swim meets felt that he had to calm and care for Mike. Mike intended it to be the other way around.

Operating rooms are very cold and grey. My memories of this moment are filled in by Mike at times. I had been drugged up beyond all reality for almost 24 hours straight. I remember

132

being lifted onto the operating table by several strong people. The sheets and screens were adjusted to cover my body. Belly exposed.

The next true memory I have is of a smell. This horrid, burning scent that made me want to throw up all the Dum Dum suckers I ate while in labor. It was curling the hair inside of my nose. I was convinced that any moment we would be evacuated for a five alarm fire in the hospital. It took me a moment to speak due to the fact it took supernatural effort for me to form words, then move my lips on purpose while producing vocals at the same time. You know those acrobats that spin plates atop metal rods? They run around in a manic state to keep several plates spinning at once without one falling and breaking? That was how busy my brain cells were commanding my voice to rise up.

"Mike,' I said in a weak voice, my face pallid in color, 'what's burning?"

"Baby, that's you."

"I'm on fire?!?"

"No baby no! Doc has a cauterizing knife so as he cuts through each layer of skin, tissue, whatever it is it sears those layers to prevent serious blood loss."

"So my layers are burning? Burn the fat off while you are in there."

I remember hearing muffled laughs and Mike saying, "Just rest baby." While he stroked my head I remember he tried to look into my eyes, but he was so fascinated with the surgery he couldn't look away. Reflecting with me later, Mike said that it was the only thing that kept him sane. He focused on the procedure before him and tried to block from his consciousness that it was happening to me.

There was tugging and pulling, I felt nauseous; a little dizzy. Then silence. No sound, no rearranging of my intestines.

My head began to list towards my left and I caught glimpse of this gigantic, butterball of a baby. He was huge! He had no neck and looked like a little old crabby man with a scrunched up face. I stared at him as he made no sound and announced to the room, "That is *NOT* my baby! Whose baby *is* that?"

No one answered me. I asked again.

"Whose baby is that?!?"

"Blondie, we are the only ones in here. He's ours. He's our baby."

I was not buying the bill of goods Mike was trying to sell me. I was told at my last round of checkups, that I would be *lucky* if my baby would weigh six pounds at birth. This chunk of a hunk weighed in at 8lbs, 9ozs and was born two weeks early. It made perfect medicinally induced sense to me that I must be on some funky baby tour and they slipped that little plump baby in there to trick me.

What I did not know in my drugged state of consciousness, was that in those moments I describe as feeling nothing and hearing nothing is what Mike was hearing and seeing.

"Let's move. Oxygen and suction."

"What's his score?"

"Zero Apgar score."

"In one minute I want an updated score."

"Yes Doctor."

Our bundle of newly birthed love was struggling to live. Mike watched our son be pulled from my body, bluish purple in color and gasping for air. He sat impotently watching his son's airways suctioned by a team of nurses and doctors speaking in numbers and medical code amongst themselves at a rapid pace.

"Start compressions. I want a score!"

"He's at a three Doctor. Color brightening up."

"Keep that oxygen on him."

The moment our son cried, and his skin began turning pink was a moment I remember. Not because I was a sober witness, but I remember hearing his cry and Mike peering at me while pulling his mask from his face to lean in and kiss me as he said, "Jen, he is crying. Do you hear him?" Mike's tears hit my cheek as he leaned over me.

That was the last thing I remember before waking hours later in recovery. I was so, so sick. Sick from so many medications, exhausted from 24 hours of labor and then a major abdominal surgery. Breathing was painful. I tried to convince my eyes to stay open and take in the movements and sounds in my room. I was back where it all began 24 hours earlier in my hospital room. Mike was standing over me and taking my surgical cap off my head. He tried to tame my hair, brushing it behind my ears.

"Baby do you want to hold him?"

I shook my head yes as tears fell down my face. Some were from pain, and some from the moment upon us. I remember looking at the clock in my room and I realized that it was almost noon and my son was almost six hours old. I still had yet to hold him in his short life outside of my body.

A clear bassinette was across the room. Mike, still in his scrubs walked over, leaned down and picked up a bundle of blankets. I heard fussing sounds from between the layers and my husband offered comforting and soothing sounds in return. He cautiously placed the baby in my arms.

I had to dig through the fabric to get to his features. I peeled the soft cotton blankets away from him. I needed to see this little face. A button nose. Thin pink lips. A dimple in his chin that no paternity test could put asunder. Small closed eyes.

I fell madly in love with this little face the moment I saw him. My sobbing was only curtailed by the pain from my incision. It hurt every time I moved. Lloyd William Tucker was born on my third wedding anniversary. I would do anything for him, including bake Mickey Mouse birthday cakes every year on this date for the rest of my life.

I took off his little hat and wanted to see if this little man had any hair. William's left side of his head was bruised, battered, slightly pushed into his skull more than his right side. He had a black eye. My heart took on such ache in an instant. My baby looked like life had sucker punched him even before he had a chance to take his first breath. I tried to talk to him through my tears.

"Wil I am so, so sorry. I would have taken that hit in the head for you a million times over if I could."

I laid my hand across his tiny chest and felt his heartbeat. I watched intently for his chest to rise and fall with each breath he took. I should have felt relieved, but I didn't. I felt guilty that already in this short time together I was unable to protect him. The first time; definitely not the last time either.

I wish ignorance was bliss, but when you study child development and it is your occupation, your mind races. Logic, hours of study and journal articles jump into your memory. You begin to go *there* with worry and *what-ifs* in your mind about your child.

As I recovered in the hospital for five more days I spoke to many a physician who peeked in on me and my son. They tried to put my mind at ease and tell me that many babies experience the same type of cranial injuries whether their birth was traumatic or not.

Years later at the age of six, Wil would be diagnosed with Apraxia. It is a motor plan disorder that affects his speech and gross motor skills. It left us puzzled for so many years. Now we knew why he was struggling in speech and other areas of development. Finally we had this diagnosis.

The area of his head that was injured at birth is the location of motor planning. This type of injury affects a number of different areas. Raising your spoon to your mouth is a motor plan. Blowing your nose successfully is a motor plan, and something that Wil could not master until he was eight years old. The brain telling words to come out of your mouth is a motor plan.

It may seem automatic in function, blowing snot into a tissue, but the body needs the capacity to talk to all of its different parts and make motion happen. Years of multiple therapists, tutors, infinitely patient teachers, specialists and aides rallied around my son made a major difference in his life. Eternal gratitude will never be an equal fulfillment of their investment in him.

His life hurdles have not always been easily cleared. He has not always been accepted in the eyes of others. He has been misunderstood and bullied. He has cried sitting in my lap because he knew he was different. He has asked me for pills that would make him smart so school would not be so hard for him.

Educators who didn't have Wil's best interest at heart have made him the talk in the hallways. People are eternally placing their foot in their mouth when they speak to me about him. Their words enter my mind, and bite hard.

"Boy you sure raised *that* one (Ryan) right."

"I don't know how you do it raising a kid *like* Wil."

"You need to find a therapy group to deal with having a son like *him*."

"Do you wish there was a place for him to go? Like *those* institutions where mentally retarded people live?"

"Can't you just get a doctor to give him something and *fix* him?"

Those instances are slashes in my soul. Those words have replayed in my head for fourteen years. They have been spoken by educators, therapists, family members, acquaintances and even friends. Some of them should know better in a professional sense; in a human being sense. When you know better, you should choose to speak carefully. Not everyone knows better, but we expect that some should. I will not lie and tell you sticks and stones may break Wil's bones but the names and morbid words never hurt him. I will not lie and tell you they never hurt his Nanny and Papa, mother, father, sister or brother either. They do.

This is also not the moment where I tell you that Wil is a victim who is misunderstood and I continually wrap him in bubble wrap to save him from the cruel world. That is not his purpose in this life, nor is it mine. I am not here to facilitate him living in the neutral corner of a boxing ring for the rest of his years. I am just the lucky one who has the opportunity to see firsthand, the man he is becoming.

That is why I tell you that even though Momma Bear in the waiting room at today's appointment wants to pounce on this person who is not treating my son with respect, I will sit tight. I will sit tight because I will not always be able to fight his battles. I don't want to fight his battles. Instead, I will take a moment, collect myself and talk with him on the drive home.

The passenger and driver doors slammed shut and I started my engine up.

"Wil, how was your appointment?"

"It was alright."

"What's wrong buddy? Do you want to talk about it?"

"Mom, I just cannot understand people…"

Oh God, here it comes. The precious words of *cheer up, find the higher road, and speak up when someone irritates* you are revving up in my mind. Where do I go? What angle do I take?

"What do you mean buddy?"

"Well, what I mean is that there was that boy sitting with his mom on the couch and they were talking in French, but I didn't understand them."

Huh?!?!? Pause. Fighting back the cackles. Okay, so Wil is not bothered by the earlier brush off. Hmm. Well, I guess I am going to take a cue and not be bothered either. Well, maybe after I have a glass of wine with Margie tonight I will not be bothered. Our conversation continued.

"Buddy how did you know it was French if you didn't understand a word they were saying?"

"I knew it was French because I recognized some of those words from SpongeBob! You know I like to listen to the episodes on my DVD player in other languages. I tried to talk with (so and so) about it during my appointment, but I don't think he gets it that you can change the languages on the videos and learn so much."

"You're right Wil. A lot of people don't get it. I get it buddy."

"I know you do Mom."

Dying to See You

I love it when a plan comes together. I love it when a project is finished. I love it when I lay 20 feet of chain in my yard that will anchor my golden stealth bombers to the ground. You are going nowhere now my little pretties!

I took all the clips, anchors and parts and lay them in the yard. I wanted to position them how they would be if both boys were outside together. I didn't want them getting tangled around a tree. I didn't want them getting tangled with each other. I wanted to make sure that there was plenty of room to do whatever it was that they needed to do outside.

Henry is the one who likes to lollygag. Perhaps that is because he has a little more meat on his bones and has no issue with taking a long inventory of the yard before settling on one spot to do his business. And then there is Jack. He is long and lean. If he was a runway model you would beg him to eat a cheeseburger.

Since Jack is so skinny he loves being outside only in the summer, and even then the love affair does not last very long. His biggest baby moments come in winter. It is not his favorite season. When you have zero fat warming your body, you would freeze your buns off too. His yelp is the most annoying thing in the world. It makes your eyelids twitch it is so shrill!

I worked and reworked my chain plotting and was happy with what I came up with. More importantly I was so proud of myself. Usually this yard stuff is Mike's cup of tea, but hey! Get a load of me working it!

The anchor needed to be screwed into the ground. It had a triangle on the top and corkscrew bottom so I twisted that baby right into the earth. No problem; bing, bang, one and done. I connected all the clamps to the chain and then the chain to the anchor.

You understand my father is an engineer and so I feel that a lot of this is genetic flow thru. I just have these talents. I cannot explain them. I came into this world knowing how to also strategically pack a car trunk for vacation too. Mike says that, "I got the smarts real good." That little dandy quote would be John Travolta talking about his massive brain power to Debra Winger in the movie Urban Cowboy.

The tale centers on Bud and Sissy, who are living the Texas dream in a troubled marriage. Sissy is looking for a real cowboy and Bud is looking for a real lady. Unfortunately they step outside their marriage looking for love in all the wrong places... They find their way back together by the end of the film – THANK GOD! One of the things that I love in the movie that I want to carry into my life, is that I want the little license plates that Bud and Sissy have in the rear window of their truck. Mike and I want to buy them for the back of his car to place in the window. Bud and Sissy respectively. I know… sappy and cheesy.

I took the other triangle anchor and was feeling really good about my last little yard project for the day. Shoot! That first one was absolutely a breeze. And yes you know what happened next. Complete and utter failure. I got the anchor halfway into the ground and then it stopped. It would not budge a bit. I went inside the house, hurriedly dug through a kitchen drawer where we already accumulated a junk.

How long had I lived here? Five minutes and already have a junk drawer? Please do not judge me.

I scooped one up, headed back out the screen door and jerry-rigged this long screwdriver through the top of the triangle to get some leverage. I got it to wiggle a little more into the dirt but not much further. What is a girl to do? Call her daddy that

143

lives 1.48 miles away of course! I gave my dad a ring and he said that he would stop by after leaving campus and twist that baby into the ground for me. He's the best.

I went inside, closed the door behind me. I was hot and needed to chill out a little bit before I went to pick up Gracie from school. The boys were already in afterschool vegetation mode on the couch. I was filling a glass with ice when my email alert on my phone blared. I moved my glass from the ice to water dispenser on the refrigerator as I fumbled for my phone in my pocket. I pulled it out and saw that it was an email from Mike. I took a big sip as I opened the email. It had an attachment and as I clicked on it to open I read the message.

"On the Ferry. Great day at the hospital. Love you baby."

Once the entire image finished opening I smiled. It was a photo of Mike onboard a ferry with some of his European coworkers on the water. He was wearing his slacks from his suit with his jacket off. Lavender colored shirt and tie to match. He didn't have a hair out of place while travelling by windy ferry. That is an obvious advantage since he shaves his head smooth.

I carried my phone and my drink upstairs to our bedroom. Closing to door behind me I headed over to the bed and propped the pillows up on my side, lay back and began to stare at the photo. I was excited to see him in real time, but felt sick to my stomach at the same time. I could see the crisp bluish skies behind Mike that faded into purples and pinks. The photo was so clear as if he had taken it with one of his paparazzi cameras. Crystal clear. It was also crystal clear tears that were welling that I could not hold back.

What is it about being the one left behind when the one you love leaves? I saw Mike's clothes hanging in the closet. I unfortunately smell his dirty socks in the laundry, yet that makes me miss him terribly. It is a constant reminder that Mike is somewhere else seeing new things and having a new experience and I am here taking in all of our familiars solo. I remain behind and see everything. When I say that I see everything I mean everything of our life together.

I felt so overwhelmed to be here without Mike. The sobs just came over me and there was nothing that I could do to calm them. I got up quickly, closed my door, and buried my head in the pillows so that Wil and Ryan would not hear me cry. The young men in my house cannot take it when I cry. They would try to cheer me up or console me, but I wanted my minute of pity.

And as I am in my pity and missing him, I get mad. I am mad at myself for getting so worked up over a photo. Mike will be home. What am I doing? What am I *doing*?

I emailed Mike back. I told him that as much as I love seeing his photo it is killing me. It rips my heart out to be away from him. Oceans are not meant to be hurdled but I really wish I had Stretch Armstrong legs right now so I could just be there in a quick hop and skip.

Tissues are never close by when you need them. I got up off my feeling-sorry-for-myself-butt and grabbed a handful from our bathroom. The worst thing after a crying fit is being so stuffy and all this snot you need to clear so you can breathe again is as backed up in your head as 5:00pm traffic in Chicago. Then you can't breathe because your sinuses are swollen from crying. This in turn makes you just want to go back to crying when you realize just what a ridiculous mess you really are.

Just when I got myself together, my phone rang. It was Mike. He could tell from my first pitiful attempt to say hello I was a hot mess.

"Baby, are you crying?"

"Stop sending me photos of what you are doing when you are doing it! I can't take it!"

145

"Please do not be upset."

"I miss you and I hate that you are so far away. I feel so stupid that I am crying and I should be thankful that I can see you. So many people are separated by miles and they *never* get to see each other. It's not like you went off to war. Oh God and some people leave and never come back!! *Why am I crying? Ugh!!!"*

"I love you so much baby. Please don't cry."

And right there and then you know that I went to the ugly cry. Mike told me not to cry, but I was gone.

I slowly got myself back together while listening to Mike talk about his day. He wanted to make sure that I had left crybaby land before he hung up. He made me laugh. He told me funny stories of the American in Germany making a constant fool of himself.

"I drove on the autobahn! It was so BLEEP-ing cool!"

He told me that it was a successful visit and with his swift and keen computer skills that he was able to save the day during a presentation.

"…and I was able to go into the files on the computer, reroute the information and BAM! The presentation worked! How 'bout that Mrs. Tucker!" Maybe he did not save the day, but I let him have his moment.

Before hanging up he made me promise not to be so upset, because it tore his heart out.

"Baby I cannot take knowing that you are home so upset and there is nothing that I can do about it. I want to fix everything. I want to make everything better. I'm still here babe. I'm always here even when I can't be there."

Yes, I know this is major *puke* and *gag me* mushy factor here. I can't apologize because that is us--truly us. We exchanged, "I love yous" and set a time for the kids to talk with him in the morning.

We hung up. I hate goodbyes and I hate hanging up.

I am not sure if I needed a nap or if the nap just took me into its enchanting embrace but the charm took me over. 20 minutes of sleep can be just the cure a big, crying mess like me needs. Before falling asleep, I was thinking about how the impact of technology today. I was comparing today to the nonexistent technology of 1992 when Mike lived in Madrid. I think both instances it was a blessing and a curse.

Today, I could instantly see what he saw on his side of the globe and connect with him via email, phone, and photograph. It felt like too much. Maybe my ignorance about how he spent his 24 hours a day in Spain had been bliss. The letters in the post box that were written then mailed in spare moments, and twice a week phone calls were bliss. Maybe that would have been better during this time too. Maybe.

A Dog's Life

There is one life principle that is proven in my home time and time again. I have a house. I have dogs. They have hair. Therefore I have dog hair in my house. Golden Retrievers have a coat that to me seems to be a bit more on the hair side than the fur side. When I think of dog fur, I think of the shorter, wiry and coarse hairs that are commonplace on a German Shepard or a Beagle. When I think of dogs that have hair I think of my boys, Sheep Dogs, Irish Setters and the like.

The older I get, the more dog fur bothers me. Not hair, fur. I will love on all types of dogs, snuggle with them and talk all sorts of jibber jabber baby talk with them and then I pay for it later. Itchy face. Itchy eyes. Itchy itches. I love them and they love me and so there is sometimes a price that is paid for this relationship.

My dogs are not allowed on the furniture. Notice I did not say my dogs DO NOT get on the furniture. I said that my dogs are not allowed on the furniture; there is a big difference in semantics, grammar and meaning.

We run a tight ship when it comes to the animals, but remember we are dealing with a butter thief and his skinny sidekick. I want to tell you more about the one canine offender who seems to get away with it more than the other. That dog with his face on the post office wall would be Henry.

I just love that sneaky lump. I truly do. His favorite place to commit unwanted slumber? The couch. When he is home, it is on the family room couch. When Henry goes to Nanny Papa's house, it is on their love seat. He is a roomy dog, and I am not quite sure how he fits on the love seat but he makes it work. I have never installed a hidden camera to see what happens, but I think it goes a little something like this.

SCENE: Early morning.

Lunches and backpacks are grabbed by Tucker children who are heading out the door to catch the school bus. Coats, kisses, and hugs are flying in the air. The man of the house is placing a pink coat on the littlest lady of the house as they make their morning commutes to day care and work respectively.

The last to leave is me. It is always me and that is a good thing. I turn off all the lights left on. I put the butter back into the refrigerator. I wipe up the counters from the morning of breakfast and lunchbox packing bombardment. I then grab my lunch, keys, sunglasses, nametag and head to the front door.

My four legged boys are usually sitting at the door by now because they have heard the jingle of my keys and think that this means something in their world. This sound usually means absolutely nothing for their daily routine, but God love them for their optimism! Jack and Henry hope that this just might be the time to go bye-bye! Here comes the pep talk. The one we have every morning.

"Jack and Henry you be good boys. Mommy loves you. Don't do anything naughty and no sleeping on furniture. I love you baby dogs. You be good!"

Door closes behind me. I see two caramel colored faces stare out the dining room window watching me get into my stretched Honda Accord to head out for the morning. Black noses pressed against the window that worked themselves between the slats in our blinds just so they can just a closer look at me as I leave. I start my auto, pop it into reverse, and take off for the day.

END SCENE

As soon as my car leaves the driveway, my dogs think that they are in the clear for whatever rousing ruckus arises. There is probably some wrestling and play-fighting over the Kong. We have three of those red rubber things you put treats in. Jack and Henry only want the one the other dog has in their possession. They do not share well.

They take a few drinks of water from their large, shared water bowl in the laundry room. There must be a quick lap around the kitchen looking for any crumbs or tiny morsels that might have hit the ground. Perhaps a plate with a half-eaten waffle was left on the kitchen table which is a reason they find to engage in immediate celebration. My money is on Henry for sneakiest table heist not in a motion picture or part of an ensemble cast. He does not need Jack's assistance for anything consumed. He does just fine on his own.

This is the point where my dogs are so exhausted for being awake for 95 minutes of the day that they need a nap. Henry bounces to the couch. Jack takes the lower bunk in Ryan's room. It's tough being my dogs isn't it?

So you are thinking right about now *Jen, if no one is home, how do you know this is what they do when you leave? How do you know they sleep on the furniture? Give them the benefit of the doubt for heaven's sake!*

I know this is fact because they have both been busted. When they are caught in the act, my dogs look at you like you are the one with the problem. Jack could sleep through anything so he does not even notice me walking into Ryan's room with my phone to get a photo of the crime to send to Mike. I snapped the

151

photo. Jack pops an ear towards me. Then slowly raises his head, and then his sleepy mug turns to look at me in the eye. He is irritated with me that I woke him up on furniture he is not supposed to be on. No words are exchanged. He gets up and not so gracefully plops to the carpet. He exits the room while snorting at me in disgust.

And then there is Henry. He is lying on the couch with his back towards me. If he had a Snuggie to wear, and the remote in his paw, this moment could be blissful for him. I quietly walk towards him in step with his snores to really get the jump on him. I am standing just inches from the couch and he has not budged. Now comes my favorite part. I get right up to his ear and say his name in sing-songy fashion.

"Hen-er-ree…"

He stirs.

He turns his head and looks over his shoulder at me.

Our eyes meet.

Henry rolls back onto his side and huffs at me, louder than a pig snorting in a mud bath. Is that the sound of disgust I hear? That I woke you on *my* couch Henry? Momma is not playing.

"HENRY! GET UP!"

I think this is the point where he has the *alright, enough already lady* thoughts percolating in his mind because unlike his brother, who has instant remorse, Henry stretches his body long and lean for dramatic effect. He lazily falls to the carpet and gives his head a good shake. He does a few downward dogs and rolls from side-to-side for one last good scratch; I clear my throat while giving him the death stare.

What would the Dog Whisperer say? Are we failures as dog parents? Do Jack and Henry need an intervention or scared straight experience? Do they have little doggie jails for things like this? Where perhaps their peers, who have done wrong in the past, convince Jack and Henry to turn back before it's too late? If they are hitting the beds and couches for a few winks each day, thinking they will never get caught then what comes next? Will they start trying to score dog treats in dark alleys? Oh the humanity…

I try to cut my dogs some slack when the alpha male is gone. Can you relate to the four-legged babies in your house knowing someone is not home who should be? They seem just as out of sorts as me when Mike is out of town. At night when everyone is tucked in bed, Jack and Henry, who usually sleep on top of each other on my or Mike's side of the bed, never come in the room with me. They sleep just outside our door facing towards the stairs. They look as if they are at the ready. I am not sure if this is a protection thing and they are on guard because Mike is gone, or if they think any moment that Daddy is going to open the front door and love on them. It is really a tossup.

So again, I have dogs and they have hair and it seems to accumulate quickly in my home. I saw some tumbleweed like hairballs rolling around my kitchen and wanted to run the sweeper before Margie and Jon came over. I am not sure if I am going to have some lovers or haters when I tell you this, but I absolutely love my vacuum! I mean I *LOVE* it! I am not sure that I love it enough to want it to accompany me on short weekend getaways, or take in the latest drink at Starbucks together kind of love. However, if there is an amorous word for one's devotion to appliances then that would define their relationship me. I stop short of calling them family members.

My vacuum was not my first love though. That was my iron. My Rowenta Power Glide Iron. It is like magic! It slides;

it marries the spray starch to shirt impeccably and really makes the task of crisp pleats a snap.

I remember an iron my mom got in the early 80's from some discount store. It was the worst memory of my teenage years! I went to a small private school and our dress code was skirts and dresses. Now my fellow Toledo Christian Eagles wear uniforms these days, and that can be no joy to iron either. Little plaid skirts with all of those pleats? No thanks! I remember using half a can of starch mixed in with the hot water spray just to iron one Forenza shirt from The Limited! And the muscle spasms in my forearm…unbelievable.

When I was in the drugged up happy place of labor with Wil, I called my friend Jill to tell her no baby yet, and somehow we happened upon this long discussion about how much I love my iron. I think she wanted baby stats and details; I gave her crease tips when ironing khaki pants. I am sure Jill thought I was a whack job! Who talks irons at a time like this? Jen Tucker does.

My second love came in the form of an aid to my kitchen. My Kitchen-Aid Epicurean Mixer. It is black. It is sleek. It is the one thing in the house that I would grab for with passionate abandon if the house was on fire besides my family. This thing has so much love to give and out of that love is birthed the most delectable baked goods. It truly is a life changer. But wait! There's more and I am not even at my vacuum yet!

I remember watching out my front window one morning for the delivery truck to arrive. I could not contain my excitement and I could not stand the wait. I was my younger self, impatiently waiting for December to tick by so St. Nick would pop down the chimney and leave the goods behind. And then there it was. The box truck pulled into my driveway. I saw in the form of two hard working guys angels sent from heaven. They installed my new love into my home and with great honor I accepted the manufacturer's instructions and warranty as if I had just been given an additional college degree leaving me with endless possibilities and limitless future.

Although grateful, I could not kick those guys out fast enough to bond with my new baby. Our little addition? *My frontloading washing machine!!!* Can you even understand my bliss? It just so happened that by the time it was installed and ready to roll that the boys came home from school. We turned it into an epic event. We threw in a load of colors, closed the door, and added the soaps and such. Sat back on the flowered rug that lay in front of it and watched.

We stared through the looking glass while mindlessly throwing down a bowl of popcorn as if we were taking in the latest matinee. It was exciting! Especially watching the different colors swim by us. We played eye spy and then chose a different article of clothing and waited for it to flash by.

How boring would doing a load of whites have been? I have avoidance tendencies when it comes to whites. I get bored folding them. It is the same color over, and over, and over, and over again. Puke! Hate it! Give me a load washed on the delicate cycle or a mass washing of blue jeans any day over whites.

We sat there for the longest time enjoying the show. Each cycle was something new and exciting!

"Did you see that?!? The water just came running down the front of the door!"

"Oooo! It's making a ton of soap bubbles now!"

"Shhh! Did you hear that? That's the water draining!"

"Eye spy with my little eye Mom's flowered bra!"

Geeks! Total appliance nerds I birthed, and I am so proud.

The last member that we brought into our appliance family is the one I was digging out of my hall closet and we like to call it in our society a vacuum. Like I said earlier, I pretty much call it family. The manufacturer calls it Sebo. It is THE best vacuum on the planet and I have been an accidental connoisseur of vacuums over the years. No one likes to have multiple experiences purchasing them. Nothing hops me up more than knowing that *they*, whoever *they* are, do not make things like they used too. So many things are created with little longevity these days. And so this little upright with extra attachments has a place of love in our family. At least I called it family, until today.

I took my little dandy of a sweeper out of the closet and as I was plugging it in decided to just sweep the kitchen and dining room floors. That is where the majority of the hairball offenders could be apprehended. Again, I have dogs therefore I have dog hair bouncing about. The hair we battle is more visible than in other places due to the hardwood floors that grace the kitchen and dining room... I flipped on the vacuum and was humming along to some Seal (you know, the singer).

He is my boyfriend, and Mike is well aware, so I am not revealing anything to cause my spouse and me to end up whipping chairs at each other on Jerry Springer. Seal is just utter hotness who can hit those notes like no other. He *truly* loves me. While belting the melody out in my own little world I was getting to the chorus of his hit, <u>I Have Been Waiting for You</u> (Can I just tell you as I typed that song title my butt cheeks were bouncing in my chair?), when I heard my Sebo make this grinding noise. I quickly turned it off and reclined it to the ground so I could look through the brush and see if something was catching. I didn't see anything particularly alarming and there was no smoky smell. No worries. I continued on my merry little way. I flipped the power back on and forged ahead. *Ugh!* That grinding noise was at it again. It was just not a constant sound, but annoying because why in the world was it happening and what was grinding?

I swept the kitchen, made it into the dining room, and was looping back around after passing by the front door. There is a nice amount of light that filters through the stained glass on the door and at certain times of the day shines onto the hardwood floor in a myriad of stripes and colors. I saw something on the floor that I thought was a little light dancing through the door, then onto the hardwoods. As I moved through the plane that would normally break the beam, I noticed the line was still there on the floor. Strange. I turned off the Sebo and crouched to the floor. And as I got closer, I didn't like what I saw. I bent down towards the floor and ran my hand over the mark. It wasn't light reflecting through the door playing a trick on my eyes.

It was a mark on the floor. Not only was it a mark on the floor, it was a mark *in* the floor!

It wasn't just a mark in the floor; it was a divot in my floor. It wasn't just a divot in my floor; it was a crater of mass proportions, length and width, in my hardwood floor. This groove was so long and deep and I couldn't figure out how in the world it had happened. Still crouching near the floor, I had a new perspective of the situation and did not like what I saw.

One after another they appeared. More of these marks. On *my* hardwoods. Some of the gashes were deeper and longer than others. My heart pounded in my ears with the pulse and beat of freshly cleaned tennis shoes taking an intensely harsh tumble in the dryer. And then it hit me. My stinking Sebo did this! Oh my gosh, how could Sebo do this to me?! I took it in. Gave it a home; a family. This is how it repays me? By trashing my floors? No! Are you kidding me?

I lay Sebo on his back to check the bottom out one more time. What I saw caused me to shutter. A tiny piece of metal was protruding from the beater bar that look like it had been bent towards the floor versus towards the machine.

157

"NO!!!!!! You stupid, stupid vacuum!"

"Mom! What's wrong?" Ryan was flying up the stairs from the family room to the kitchen towards me.

"I am gonna beat this hunk of junk! Look at my floors!!"

Ryan paused. Looked at me then his gazed moseyed toward Sebo; the former love of my life. He grimaced as I told him what happened to the floors. I think I was whining at this point. Toddler whining. The toddler whining that resembled you not buying me Goldfish crackers in the checkout line at Target type of whining.

He came over to me; I am still sitting on the floor. My head down in my hands; head shaking back and forth. It think I was moaning words with no understanding what in the world I was saying. This was Ryan's moment. He could shine as man of the house and give me advice. Ease my woes and comfort me. Be my comforter in his father's absence. Step up and give me a moment of compassion that I needed, because short of sanding all my flooring, I will now be residing with eight, yes eight monumental crevasses in my home. Foxholes for field mice. That's what they are now!

"Mom," Ryan gently lifted my chin with his thin fingers and looked me in the eye. I looked into his baby blues while biting my lip to keep it together and not cry. My young man was about to make me feel better. For so many years it mostly was the other way around, but now maybe the baton is passing. Maybe he is seeing me as a real flesh and blood human being and not just Mom. Ryan was one of the "men of the house" with Mike gone. This could be the destined point that Ryan persuades me to come out of this funk with words of wisdom. He would draw upon the coping tools that have been imparted to him over the years from his loving parents. I could not wait for him to speak and make me feel better.

"You know that *stupid* is a bad word, right Mom?"

Thank you Ryan, Thank you. That was just the little nugget I was hoping for.

Here I Come to Save the Day!

I walked over to the stairs and had a seat. It was either that or go up to my room and cry again, but that option was *not* an option since any minute Jon and Margie were going to ring the bell. Stupid Europe! Stupid Sebo! There! I said it *again* and I said it *twice*! STUPID!!!

Don't get me wrong. I am so glad that my kids still think that stupid is a bad word. I know my boys have heard worse. I'm not sure what it's like in your home, but in our house if I get called out about my language and it revolves around that particular "S" word, and not the other one we as a "global people" usually refer when speaking of the "S" word, then I am okay with that.

From this vantage point on the stairs, I could see two things. The first thing catching my eye was three of the moon sized craters in my hardwoods, and the second was my dad pulling into the driveway. How do daddies know when to show up? Even when we are no longer crying from skinned knees or missing a Barbie roller skate, somehow they just know.

I am just shy of 40 and yet I am still my daddy's little girl. The princess. There is a scene in the movie Father of the Bride, the version starring Steve Martin and Diane Keaton in the early 90's when their daughter Annie returns and after a European romance with a young man. She tells her parents that she is getting married. Steve Martin looks at his daughter through the eyes of a father seeing his little girl as a six-year-old with pigtails. Not as the young woman who actually is in his presence. I know that is *exactly* how my dad sees me even today. Mike and I joke about Jen Tucker being the only virgin with three children she birthed on the planet. Can you relate? My dad is a very intelligent man, but he must think that my pregnancies were either the result of a dirty toilet seat, or a public pool mishap. You never know what could happen if the chemicals are not strong enough in the water. I am just saying...

The irony continues in my own little family. It is funny how Mike sees our sons versus his daughter. He has already taken a hypocritical giant leap for mankind when talking about his hopes and dreams for his sons versus his daughter.

Mike wants the boys to hurry up and get to college, get out of the house, get jobs and get girlfriends. Gracie, on the other hand, may never date while her father is alive. Purdue University has a winter sports event called the Nude Olympics. Neither myself, nor my spouse, ever took part in this ritual. On one of the coldest nights of the year, undergraduates shed their clothes and run the Carey Quadrangle in all their birthday suit glory. Mike said he would cheer his sons on in the event. He would even throw them some clothes to put on followed with an "atta boy" slap on their backs. Gracie, on the other hand would be impounded for all winter months on the calendar as a preventative measure. No parole even for good behavior.

I think that it was our first night home from the hospital with Isabella Grace where this mental shift of being the father of a daughter first happened for Mike. I remember coming home, letting our dog Theo smell and love on his new baby, and then taking her up to her room for a tour. Gracie was in need of a fresh diaper and so we spent time together singing and talking,

162

her mostly sleeping and listening, and having our first moment together in her room.

I was fastening up the sides of her freshly cleaned drawers, when Mike entered her celery and pink colored dwelling. He was pale. He didn't speak at first and I just stared at him waiting for something to come out of his mouth because the look on his face told me there were about a million words in there just yearning to get out. And then, it happened.

"Did you know that Halle Berry is someone's daughter?"

Como?

I just looked at him. Like he was a total idiot.

He reiterated a little stronger in tone still working the theory in his head as if he had just made this discovery working along Henry Ford or Albert Einstein. Eureka!

"Did you *know* that Halle Berry is *someone's* daughter?!"

"I did know that Mike. Are you just realizing this fact?"

Mike just looked at me and was freaked to the core.

"Do you know that Halle Berry has a father? He would be really upset with me knowing the things I thought about his daughter, because one day Isabella is going to be a woman and men will think things about her. Things like the things I think about Halle Berry. I will never, *ever* think that way about her again! It's wrong. *Just so wrong!*"

Mike looked at me, and then at his daughter who was awake at this moment, lying on the changing table. He then backed out of the room all the while maintaining us in his visual.

Wow! I think we just had quite a moment there. To laugh at Mike to his face was not an option so I waited and did it behind his back after he walked backwards out of the room. I heard the door of our master bedroom close and I could not hold the laughter in another second! I would have bust a gut literally

163

since I was recovering from a cesarean section, so I tried to keep it down to a low snicker.

Gracie's room housed the black walnut rocking chair that once belonged to Mike's Grandmother, and then to his mother Evie, and now it was in our home. We gently sat down together on the pink toile cushions and I laid my daughter to my chest. I smoothed the ruffles on her dress. I whispered words of comfort while she began to drift back into slumber. Little Ella Gracie snuggled in just under my ear and into my neck.

"Man I really feel sorry for you that your Daddy is a complete nut job, Ella. I truly am. He is only like this because he is nuts about you. Don't ever forget that you are someone's daughter. Albeit a whacko's daughter. Your daddy loves you so, so much."

I closed my eyes and patted her small back. She did not have much hair on her head, but I rubbed my fingers though what little bits were there.

"We will get through the years with Daddy together my love. You, me and Halle Berry…we will all make it through together. Just the three of us."

This was a moment where my husband understood how much my father was nuts about me, was amped up just a teensy bit more.

And now this present moment would be marked in time as the moment my Daddy came to save me from my runaway dogs. I hopped up from the stairs to get to the door as he was ringing the doorbell. I always greet him with a big hug and kiss, unless he has some kind of creeping crud, sick germs that I would rather not share.

"Hey Daddy (yes I am about to hit 40 years young, and call my dad, Daddy), thanks so much for coming over. How was your day?"

"Great! I am not in charge anymore!" Remember my dad just "stepped up" into faculty from being the department head of his school for just shy of a decade. Purdue was just getting back into the swing of the fall semester.

We wandered through the house and I took him through the kitchen then out the door to the yard and showed off the beginning stages of my handiwork.

"I got the anchors screwed down really well on this run, but this one didn't want to go all the way into the ground. I tried the long screwdriver thingy as leverage, but that is as far as it would budge."

It was sticking up a good two inches from the surface of the soil.

My dad scratched his chin. Gave it the Inspector Gadget once over and sent me to fetch the long screwdriver I had used earlier. I handed it to him and he gave it about half a turn when it became stuck for him as well. Dad switched his hands around a little bit and tried to gain a little momentum. Not happening. He stood up, wiped his brow with a handkerchief. He always carries one. "Man! That baby does not want to budge."

He went back at it, this time breaking a sweat. There are times I hate seeing my dad work hard, and for some reason this was one of them. I know my dad is not fragile. Anyone who goes to the doctor for a head cold, who never goes to the doctor by the way, and leaves finding out he has stage four colon cancer and prostate cancer, then beats it a few months later by changing his diet and lifestyle after surgery is no wuss. No chemo; no radiation. He is a tough guy. But I still worry.

I have entered a second set of "tween years." No one warned me about them coming my way. The first set was my middle school years. Everything was awkward. Braces and pimples make you feel like your face is full of landmines, and your smile looks like Jaws from the 007 Roger Moore era. Growing out my sandy blonde hair from the Pat Benetar short chop, into a choppy bob was not really my "cover girl" time. You think that might be *it* in life. You might think, *if I can just get out of this segment of my life, then I will be okay.* I made it out of those tween years, and somehow find myself back there now. Not with headgear and Oxy cream this time. This time, it is very different.

I have now hit the second tween stage of life. I am at that stage of existence where I feel the baton of life has been handed to me from my parents. I am now the parent for my parents. I worry about them. I make them call me when they are out too late. I make them call me when they arrive at their said destination after a long drive or flight across the states. I ask my mom if she has refilled her blood pressure medication and what the doctor says about scheduling knee replacement surgery.

I make sure that my dad "airs" himself out while working on campus and goes for a breezy walk rather than staying cooped up behind his email inbox all day. There was no ceremony. No royal decree. This shift just happened where I now feel I worry about my parents more than they could ever worry about me. If you factor in the only child aspect, then I am doubly screwed with worry for them. It is just me. I have no siblings to share this feeling with. Mike is a huge help and loves my parents beyond measure. He has sisters. He doesn't understand. It truly is just me.

I can tell you that once my last grandparent had passed away, I had the epiphany of my parents' mortality. I can tell you that making the drive several times a week for many months to sit with my dad, and make grocery runs for my mom during his battle with cancer forced me to make peace with the beast of his diagnosis.

Maybe saying that I made peace with cancer is not the right way to say it. I needed to make peace with the fact that if my dad died from this situation, this family robber (cancer), that his healing was in heaven. It was not meant to happen here on earth. That was not something I accepted easily. It only happened on one of my hour and a half drives from West Lafayette when we lived in Indianapolis. I found it in the throes of sobs, on a rainy trek home, listening to silence.

I could not take the voices of radio.

I could not talk to a soul on my phone.

I could not pretend that I was hanging tough.

I was sick of talking about it.

I wanted God to fix my dad and fix him now!

My dear friends will tell you that these were the days I became a hermit. That was never a descriptor of Jen Tucker. I was dealing with my father's illness. On top of that, I was dealing and healing from years of gluten eating away my insides. I had been diagnosed with advanced Celiac Disease shortly before my dad's cancer diagnosis and lived every day feeling like a weed whacker fed on my intestines.

My energy was low. No Energizer Bunny fed me strength. My daddy needed me and I felt so physically and emotionally ill, that what little I had to give was all for him. No one else. My children got the scraps and Mike had slim to none of me. I was a mess. A controlling mess that came to the lightning bolt revelation that there was nothing I could do for my

167

daddy. *Nothing. Nothing I could do*! I can't cure cancer. I can't play God. I can't see straight because I have turned myself into *this*. What good was I truly doing anyone in such a state?

Do you have any idea how incredibly defeating, and at the same time releasing it is to admit my inadequacies? I felt like I had lost the battle. What I gained however was the fortitude that I was ready to now say to God what He knew all along.

My dad was His. My daddy had always been His. I was trying to take my dad from Him and fix him with logic and grocery shopping and holding his hand. I was trying to fix my dad by telling him only a witch doctor would tell him not to have chemo or radiation. If you have cancer that is what you do! You go once a week and have doctors inject the meds that kill the bad cells, unfortunately the good cells perish as well. Then we work towards getting better with all these herbs and acupuncture needles. That is what I thought you did because that was all I knew.

That was all I knew because I did not put my father in the hands of The Great Physician, our Heavenly Father. Once I confessed my fears and gave my dad back to his God, the swell of comfort I felt was more than I can speak of. Never had I felt so enveloped in love and compassion.

This is not to say I have never worried again. That would be a big, fat lie. What I do know is this. My dad is here for a purpose. He is my hero and rock. When it is time for him to commence his journey home to heaven and laugh again with his best friend who beat him there, Harold Meaux, then I can say oh happy day. I will see him in eternity.

But right now, I am seeing him drip all over his boilermaker attire with perspiration. Putting the last spin on the screwdriver to forever affix my dogs to the yard.

"Jenny I think that I have that baby all tightened up, but I think that I should wrap the anchor in duct tape. That will keep it secure and then no dogs will escape to run the neighborhood."

Did he just say duct tape?

"Dad,' my hands on my hips, channeling my inner mouthy 13 year old (or maybe it was me imitating Gracie from earlier in the day), 'That is ridiculous! The dude said at the hardware store that this will withstand over 800 pounds of pressure with all the components combined! Don't wrap it in duct tape. That's just crazy! And unattractive!"

My father laughs at me. I knew that would happen from my unattractive comment.

"Well, I just want to make sure no one goes anywhere."

"They won't Dad. I think we are good."

Seriously?! Duct tape? Never send in an engineer to do a yard designers job. I've got to get Bob Herrick to quit watching the western channel and expand his horizons with a little HGTV!

Margie is Here!

My Dad was just finishing up, when into the driveway rolled Jon and Margie Story. You have no idea how happy I was to see that Jeep roll up to my house!

Seriously happy!

I went outside and we greeted each other with big hugs, big kisses and then we started to haul food inside. I felt like we looked like a line of ants carrying our prized finds to place into the communal safe place of winter storage. One thing about my friend Margie, if she says she's going cook for you…she is going to do some serious cooking!

It is no small feat to cook for a bunch of gluten intolerant people, but know this, Margie will *never* have to ask me twice to make me dinner. She makes it look like a piece of wheat free cake. There is a fine art to cooking for a Celiac and it can be intimidating for sure. You worry about the taste. You worry about cross contamination with gluten items. And then there are the hidden glutens that people worry about when reading ingredient labels. My friend has a certain finesse, and also is married to a food and nutrition guy. Margie had better not accidently kill me with wheat, or it would make Jon look really bad come his yearly review and salary increase.

So just to be clear, there is no conversation between Margie and I where she sweetly offers to cook for my family and I decline. She does not need to insist, and then I say it is a bother for her to go to such great lengths. She does not badger me into cooking for my family.

Not even a onetime refusal leaves my mouth. I am not sure she even gets the full sentence out with her request before I whip out my cell phone and punch up my calendar to decide on a date.

I asked my dad if he and Mom would like to come over and have dinner with us. I was not worried at all that there wouldn't be enough food to go around. There was plenty!

One huge tray full of chicken, with each piece blanketed with a slice of swiss cheese, a dollop of sour cream, and then a hint of color with green avocado on top. There were phenomenal cheesy potatoes, freshly blanched green beans, a gelatin that bounced with berries inside, and the delicious banana pudding with whipped cream, mini chocolate morsels and a few nuts sprinkled atop. Hungry yet?

The biggest concern of what would be shared while breaking break in my home was how much wine Margie brought. For I am a chip off the old block when it comes to enjoying a glass of vino, and if there was not enough to share with my mom, well then that was the deal breaker. I love my mother to pieces, but you must understand that I have needs. My need right then and there was a nice, non-rationed glass of the grape. I really do share well with others, but not today!

My Dad left us for a bit and drove the short 1.48 miles to pick up my mom and bring her back over for dinner. While he was gone, Margie and I caught up on our day's events as she put the finishing touches on dinner and I set the table.

I think at this point my sons had roped Jon into checking out some manly something around the house. This could vary from a gadget, to an episode of SpongeBob, to God only knows. I have to tell you that I am so blessed to have this woman and her husband in my life. It will be 19 years this May that I have known Margie and to say that she is important in my life is an understatement.

I have a short list of go-to-gals. I have so many dear people in my life that I love to spend time with, laugh with, dine and story tell with. I have also been blessed with women in my life, who are there for me, and I mean selflessly *there* for me and Margie is such a person. We all need people like that in our life, right? We need people who can know all the bad stuff about us but who still want to be around us.

She is someone who knows everything about me. No secret will be revealed on a tabloid that would shock her and yet she still loves me. The only thing she might not know could possibly be... Hmm... Nope! Nada! Not one!

Margie is just a smidgeon older than I am. I will never tell you how old, but know that our relationship started when I was an undergraduate, newlywed who was given the task of student teaching in her classroom. Margie's twin daughters and son were in college or heading that way. She was a 9 year-old child bride. That seems to be how they do it in Iowa I guess.

Margie and I had so much fun the semester that I taught with her. We decided early on that we needed to eat out once a week at lunch time just to make sure that I was doing okay and we were on the same page of where I stood during my final leg of earning my degree.

I am sorry to tell any of my fellow early childhood education majors the following news that spent time with Margie during their four years at Purdue. I will be honest with you–I am her favorite student teacher ever. Sorry, but true. She loves me best and if you have a different version of my delusion then I would be most appreciative if you would simply keep that little thought to yourself.

Perhaps you are under the impression that she was partial to you. That you were the Head Teacher's Pet. Hate to burst your bubble, but honestly she just wanted to see you achieve and do your best work and not destroy your fragile ego as you finished your final year of college. She would never tell you that because that is the kind of Margie she is. Know this...I win!

Okay, okay in all seriousness Margie is a nurturer who comforts and loves many. Although she is no longer teaching preschoolers, except with me on Sundays at church, Margie has moved into a student advisor roll on campus that absolutely suits her. Her students are lucky to have such a treasure to support and encourage them through this time of self-searching growth, beer swilling, and cutting class.

I am sure that when she feels like smacking them upside the head when they try to explain away their debilitating grades, she looks at the photos of her darling granddaughters and prays for them to just have an extra dose of smarts. The smarts that some of her students might need.

Margie is timeless. She just does not age. I know right now she is saying *yeah right Jen!* She is just a gorgeous creature inside and out. I am constantly lusting after her shoes too. We have very similar taste when it comes to clothing. Give me a great t-shirt and hoodie and we will be good to go! A little relaxed and hip, but nothing with a heel please unless it is a Dansko clog. Now if I can just get her to order her shoes a little too big on accident, I could hit the big time.

We sat at our dining room table, which seemed so empty to me even with eight people joined together there. It is always missing the most important guest when Mike is gone. Laughter billowed. Anecdotes brought tears. Gracie entertained. The golden retrievers made their rounds looking for the super suckers who would sneak them a snack under the table. Wine glasses were full. Dinner was served with a mountainous helping of joy.

The dogs were becoming a little too friendly while trying to dine, so my dad offered to put them outside on the chains. Jack, my streamlined, boney love likes to rest his chin on the crook of your arm as I shared with you before. As you try to lift the spoon to mouth, cut a piece of meat, type on the computer. It is a little cumbersome. Obviously, not to him.

Henry just bursts from under the table to rest on your lap with his nose and eyes meeting yours. They like to use their wit and charm to beg for food. What can I say? It is a life skill. We were much better, stricter doggy parents with Theo. Since Jack and Henry were adopted as two-year-olds there are some things that we overlook. I can also bring it back to the different way you parent your first child than you might parent the third. For example, when Wil was a baby he was only allowed to crawl in our small family room freely with Mike or me with him. If he wanted to crawl around the house, we followed right behind him to the point of tripping over him if he stopped too quickly. Then came Ryan, and we knew we had put all the pretty things up high, put safety plugs in the outlets, the doors were locked and we didn't worry as much. Ella Gracie arrived and she had the run of the house. Our conversation would revolve around the last time we saw her crawling around. If Mike had seen two episodes of Judge Judy since the last sighting, it might be time to figure out where she was in the house.

The smells were a little much for Jack and Henry. My dad took the lads out to their chains and rejoined us. Our conversation turned to the construction next door. This has so much irony for so, so many reasons.

Reason #1: Mike and I have lived in two different neighborhoods with new construction. We had lived our fill of nails in car tires. We heard too many saws buzzing at 7:00AM on a Saturday morning. We loved those communities, however wanted a different, more mature neighborhood.

Reason #2: We chose an older, established neighborhood for the property, the mature trees, and no new construction. Guess where the only lot left to build on, that had been for sale for over 30 years was located in our neighborhood? Yep! Right next door to us. Guess when building began? Building commenced as soon as we signed on the dotted line owning our house. No reflection on our new neighbors whom we enjoy dearly, but seriously what are the odds? So crazy!

The house was really coming along and we saw one of our sweet neighbors walking her dog and checking out the construction site. I should say the others at the table watched out the window. My head was buried in my plate of yum. I heard Margie chime in, "Jen, does your neighbor have a golden retriever too?"

My eyeballs were the only thing to pop up from my plate in her direction. "No, she has that beautiful, black lab that is barking at that other dog. I don't know whose…"

No. NO! *NOOOOOOOOO!* It was *my* golden retriever Henry, barking his tail off at my neighbor's dog and trailing behind him; ten feet of chain. Escape from Alcatraz had nothing on my dog.

I stood at the window in my dining room and felt utterly betrayed by the metal links that were to keep him from such an evasion. I was stunned. How could this have happened? Is my dog bionic? Was he really the pet of Steve Austin or Jamie Sommers? Had Henry escaped after his Terminator parts where installed and that is why he has such super canine strength? Who are you Henry Tucker? You are a foodie, who rips chain apart in a single bound!

I looked at my dad. Dad looked at me. I walked to my garage and dug through the drawers and found what I needed to fix this situation. Returning to the dining room I handed the only thing that could save us over to my dad; the duct tape.

My Soul is Cake

When you close the door behind the last loved one to leave it is two-fold. On one hand you are thinking of that amazing time we had together. It obviously defied the strength of metal alloys. You reflect on the electable dinner with humorous and vivacious conversation. It was a lovely evening. On the other hand, it is now over. Dinner with friends and family, but most importantly this day. What a day! So glad it is almost over!!!

Margie had helped me tidy up the kitchen and put the leftovers in containers. I rinsed plates and loaded up the dish washer and was wiping down the counters when I realized that it was almost 8:30 p.m. Definitely time for Gracie to be in bed. I gave the dishrag a toss on the counter, and decided that tis a far, far better thing to get the gremlin in bed ASAP, and finish the dishes in the solitude that would follow. There is nothing worse than a sleepy, crabby Gracie at the rooster crow. No one wants to be exposed to such pain and atrocity that Gracie spews in the throes of her drama. Especially before the sunrise. It's too much.

I walked up the stairs and was floored. Literally. I tripped over my own feet walking up the stairs. How embarrassing. Seriously? Even trying to go to bed the hits keep on rolling?

Usually I only do that when I am bombarded by a retriever getting under foot. What I really hate is when my toes get caught up in my pajama pant leg! I like those yoga pants that fit tightly through the leg to the knee and then flair slightly to the seam. Almost every time I wear those stinking pants, somehow my foot gets all caught up in the extra fabric that hovers over my toes. With each stair step I take, I am destined and aware that I might trip like a baby learning to maneuver the incline.

I don't know why, but I always take a look around to make sure no one saw me; especially my children who would rejoice in my foot folly. Luckily I was off the hook; no witnesses! It never happened. You got my back right?

I checked on Wil who was in his bathroom scrubbing and polishing his braces and teeth to a shiny tin grin. Wil is taller than I am. I hate it. He hates how much I emphasize the fact that Mike once carried him cradled in his right arm like a football. He hates it when I ask him to never leave me, *ever*. I want Wil, as well as Ryan, to live with me forever. I don't *really* mean it though. Well, maybe I mean it just a little. Wil always kisses me on the forehead and sends me on my way. I remember when it was once the opposite. I was the kisser and he was the kissee, but even in heels I cannot reach his hair line to smooch.

Ry was in his top bunk reading. That is his designated reading spot. Not the bottom bunk where he sleeps. I *love* that he is a book worm and it is a passion he shares with my mom, his Nanny. He even adopted the bookcase that was once my mom's. It kept her periodicals all neatly organized. Her grandfather crafted it for her when she was quite young.

The bookcase went from stained wood to a Martha Stewart Blue Suede Shoes color once it became Ryan's, but the purpose is cyclical. All he has to do is call my mom and mention "book store," and they hit the road together. I keep trying to tell them both that there is this amazing place we call a *library*, where you can just go get books and borrow them. For free! They both look at me like I am deranged. Borrowing them must be inferior for some reason that I do not understand.

My mom was trying to make more space in her bookcases that surround the fireplace in their family room one time when I told her that she really had so many books that it would be a great idea to donate those to a school or library where others could enjoy them. She looked at me with a melting glare.

"*You* want *me* to give away my *friends*?!"

The woman who gave me life wanted me dead. I had no idea that she and her hardcovers had this type of relationship with each other. I thought I knew most of my mom's friends. Wow! Just when you think you really know someone.

When I tell you that my mom has a lot of books, err...*friends*, I mean she literally has boxes, and boxes, and boxes, and shelves, and shelves full of friends. I think it might be a felony to lock your friends in a box in your attic though. Ryan is different. He has some books he reads, and he is ready to donate them to a school or a charity that works with children. Others have a great place of love and honor on his bookshelf; my mom's former friend-shelf. Ryan's most prized book would be the one signed by Drew Brees.

My mom found out that Purdue football great and Saints Quarterback Drew Brees would be in town signing his new book, and she was excited! She called the boys and told them that she was going to pick them up and they would make a day of it. Ryan could not wait to be in the same room, taking up the same space as one of his hero quarterbacks.

"Mom, I think I am gonna pass out when I see Drew."

"Well Ry, you need to think of something to say to him. You will not have a lot of time to talk, but I am sure you could say something."

"There is nothing I could ever say to him. I would puke!"

I tried to be cool and just think strategy.

"You need a conversation starter."

"A what?! What would I say to Drew Brees because he is *Drew Brees?"*

"Well… You could ask him if the Drew Brees Favorite Breakfast at Triple XXX is *really* his favorite meal there, or if it's made up."

There was a twinkle in my boy's eye.

"Mom! That's a great idea! Do you have any others?"

Did he just say I had a great idea? I need to Polaroid this moment in my mind for future reference.

"You know Ry, you can tell Drew that you know Kitch (Our good buddy Kelly Kitchel). He played football with Drew at Purdue and they are still great friends. You have that in common!"

Ryan looked at me with a look I had not seen in a long time. Eyes smiling wider than his lips.

"Mom you are *genius*! Oh man this will be great! Thanks Mom!"

Ry gave me a kiss on the cheek and ran out of the room. I was not really in the moment relishing the kiss, but living in the previous one that had my name and the word *genius* in it. The fact that those words were uttered by my preteen angst ridden son, who usually finds me clueless was a split-second to behold.

I remember that the entire time Ryan and Wil were with my mom I was on pins and needles. I would check the time and could not wait to hear them walk in so I could get the entire scoop. I sent Kitch a text telling him about how I pumped Ryan up to meet Drew, and even he was waiting to hear the results of said interface. Just as a watched pot boils at a snail's pace, so did the minutes off the clock. I was so excited for Ryan. How often do we have the opportunity in this life to come face-to-face with someone you look up to, admire? Someone you want to emulate. My excitement for him was big time.

181

Four *looooooooooong* hours after they left, I heard the front door open and slam shut. I was upstairs folding laundry and yelled for the boys to come up and see me. Ryan came up and leaned in the doorway. I didn't like his body language. It didn't look like a boy who just met the man that makes my boy a Saints fan.

"Hey Mom."

That's it. That's all he had for me was "Hey Mom?" I thought he would be talking a mile a minute!

"Well how was it buddy?"

"It was okay."

Huh?!? I think that the descriptor that I was looking for was bigger than just *okay*.

"It was *okay*? What do you mean? Didn't you see Drew?"

"Yeah I did. We waited a long time and he signed my book, Wil's book, one for Nana and one for you. Nana got an extra too just in case someone needs one or something."

I paused. I was waiting for this explosion of dialog to commence and I felt like I was pulling words from a mute!

"Well did you say anything to him? Did you ask him about his meal at Triple XXX or tell him you know Kitch?"

I couldn't take it! I was on pins and needles. Ryan didn't answer me. He just stood there shuffling in his shoes and staring at the carpet. Finally he broke the silence.

"Mom, I said nothing. I couldn't speak. I mean he is **Drew Brees** Mom! Do you know that? But I tried Mom, I really did. I couldn't make any words come out of my mouth."

Ryan finally looked up at me and I walked over to him, putting my hand on his moppy head and gave it a tussle.

"Ry I am so glad you got to see Drew. That is really cool. Did he say anything to you?"

Ryan smiled, "Yeah he did! He said, 'You're welcome bud.'"

I perked up and said, "Well you had to have said *something* to him, so you did talk to him! What did you say?!"

"Nana elbowed me and made me say 'thank you.'"

And so there you have it. My son Ryan, and his deep and meaningful conversation with Purdue greatness, and Super Bowl MVP Drew Brees. And now this Boilermaker's book will be another friend on my mother's bookshelf but will have a place of honor in my son's. Where my mom's *friends* once resided in her childhood bedroom, a wonderful memory of a moment in time rests on the same shelves that now belong to my son.

I gave Ryan the 15 minute warning that it would be time to switch to the sleep bunk, and he gave me a wink and a hug around the neck. I walked from Ryan's room into Gracie's, and since they have a wall that boarders their rooms, it's not that long of a haul. When I stepped into her room, I could hear her giggles coming from under her comforter. She really is not the best at trying to hide. More than her giggles giving her away, is the fact that she left a Gracie shaped lump and outline under her flowered comforter revealing her whereabouts. Not to mention her stringy blonde hair popping out. Dead giveaway. I threw back the covers and was met with precious merriment. There are no better sweets to my ears than the echoes of my children's laughter.

I cuddled Gracie into my lap and gave her what seemed like endless kisses. I love this time in the evening with her. We talk about our respective days a little more, we read stories together, and then we say prayers, followed by our blessings for others.

> *Now I lay me down to sleep,*
> *I pray The Lord my soul to keep.*
> *If I should die before I wake,*
> *I pray The Lord my soul to take.*

That is the prayer I affirm. Here is Gracie's version:

> *Now I lay me down to sleep,*
> *I pray The Lord my soul to tape.*
> *If I should die before I wake,*
> *I pray The Lord my soul is cake.*

Isn't that what we all wish? That God would tape the parts of our wounded souls together and make them as delicious to Him as cake? I know that I long to be sweeter at my core than I feel at the surface of my skin. This prayer so beautifully reflects the yearning that I feel to be sweet to the nucleus of my being, and have it radiate each and every day.

I know I fall short. I am definitely not perfect. We come into contact with so many hurtful distractors than can become like a hole punch into our spirits. Some are misunderstandings, misinterpretations, misrepresentations of our authentic selves and others. It can leave holes that no other entity can truly fill. If we allow Him, how beautifully our Maker can heal our heartbreak and trauma, and bind our weary soul's vitality back together and better than ever. The trick is you must let Him do so.

So Gracie says her version, and I say mine and we end at the God Bless portion of prayer. I love to hear the things on her mind that roll off her tongue. The incidents in her day that cause her to mention them to God. This is a time I try to be silent and let her requests be made known.

"God bless Nanny Papa, Wil and Ry Ry, Happy Puppies (that would be Jack and Henry), and the kitty cats that need homes. God bless my teachers and the sick and the sad. God bless Daddy and his airplane. God bless first class and Netflix on the channels. God bless his food and the five dinners he eats on the plane. God bless My Little Pony and when the ponies fly don't let them crash into Daddy's airplane. God bless Mommy because she needs it to not miss Daddy so much. God bless Margie because she brought me green Cheetos. God bless Allie (Gracie's BFF) and her baby Megan. God bless Mingy (My sweetest friend Mary who has known me through Barbies, braces, bras, and college bars) and her Bejeweled games on her phone and don't let her phone break when I see her so I can play. Amen! Oh! And I almost forgot, God bless the Easter Bunny so that he can make all the chocolate I can eat. Amen!"

I always think about how her prayers are innocent and to the point and mine can tend to be so heavy and wordy sometimes. Should we really be blessing first class meals and Netflix? We should bless the meals that others eat and the movies we watch even if we are bitter, standing in our kitchens cooking dinners that our kids will not eat while wearing yoga pants.

I am glad Gracie has that perspective because the night before I was too caught up in my own married single parent misery to think about blessing five course meals and airplane seats that recline flat.

I kissed her sweet forehead and her arms embraced my neck. I could stay like that forever, but my lower back would revolt, so we kissed again and said good night. Although, it is not really the final *good night* with her. I will see her in my bedroom in a few hours. Gracie will end up in bed with me later in wee hours, and the experience is like sleeping with a spider that crawls all over you. I bet it is a sleeping ritual we might share right? I think of it as the slumber party from Hell. There is no slumber, only me trying to line my side of the bed with pillows to keep her away. And why in the world does she get so close to me in a king size bed? Isn't there enough space to go around? Yes, I love her arms around my neck and when we are cheek to cheek, but her foot in my back is not cool. Not cool at all.

52 Pick Up

The last thing to clean up of our wonderful evening together was the napkins on the dining room table. Even if the rest of my house is in disarray, there is something to me about having this room looking great and clutter free, which is rare but I try. Most likely because it is the first room that you see when you walk in the door. It is all downhill in my house after that room though I tell you.

I keep the napkins in a cutie pie, silver toned, lemon patterned holder that holds the napkins up vertically on my kitchen table. *Standing at attention and ready to serve at all times* is the motto of each napkin that lives in our home. They live a life on the edge.

One might grace a lap, blow a nose, capture eye goo from my dogs, or hold splatter from sauce that graced one's face. Those napkins, if I would let them, would be the type not to keep their feet behind the yellow line waiting for the next ride at an amusement park. If they could drive a sports car, it would be the James Bond version of the Aston Martin. Those babies are in and out doing their job like a super spy! Reinforcements are always close by incase there is a need for back up. They serve quickly and serve well.

I just love napkins, or *mackins* as my Ella Gracie calls them. Napkins and perhaps all paper products live on the edge really. Called upon to perform quick and dirty duty. There is no seat belt for them keeping them in their seats at all times. I never really thought they ever needed one, until this moment. It was like a train wreck you can do nothing to stop. It was like the milk that spills all over the dining room table in super slow motion that you cannot rewind and remedy. The napkins fell from the napkin holder that was in my hand in rhythmic fashion like some sort of bizarre synchronized skydive. They hit the floor; all of them. I stared at the napkins. They stared at me. I stared at them. They stared at me. Good night napkins on the floor. See you in the morning. Thanks for keeping the floor warm, since that is now an obvious part of your duties tonight. I bet you won't need your Aston Martin for that now will ya.

I WANT TO GO TO BED! ALL DONE WITH THIS DAY!!!

Anyone Have a Straight-Jacket?

Run away dogs twice-over. Listening to someone ignore my son. Dry cleaning that forgot to get cleaned. Termites doing the backstroke in my floors. Napkins that pulled the rip cord too early. Crying from emails and photos. This day is almost over!

I flopped on my bed and stared at the ceiling. I was spent. I was tired. I missed Mike. A lot of people have a night time routine before they call it a day. There is a certain order you might do things in before you hit the sack. I know that I have certain things I do in my repertoire, but never in any order. There is always the brushing of the teeth and medicines I take, but everything else is optional. Flossing; optional. Scrubbing of my make-up; optional. Scanning my chin and neck for stray hairs to pluck; optional with the note to recheck in the morning.

The longer I lay there, the longer I did not want to move. My mom describes it this way. The older you get, the harder it is to get your body to do the things you want it to do. So you have to talk to your body. Encourage it to take action and move towards motion. That would be me it this very moment.

The only caveat being that I have to actually get the will power to want to talk with my body to make it move. And so this great debate rages on, until I realize that the longer I talk myself out of getting up, the longer it will be to hit the pillow for the night.

My feet hit the floor and I headed into the bathroom. I opened up my medicine chest and took out my night-night candy and no baby pills. The "night-night candy" would be a little Tylenol PM that I take every night before I go to bed. I have some discs that are disappearing from my spine and if I wake up in the middle of the night on my back, I am in too much pain usually to just roll over and go back to sleep. I have also entered the phase of life where if I wake up at 3:00AM to pee, any and every thought known to mankind has the possibility to enter my mind and force every bit of returning to slumber out of the picture. So, as my friend Jocelyn has coined the phrase, it is my night-night candy. I popped those little, blue babies out of the package and chased them down my throat with a sip of water.

The no baby pills? Well those should be self-explanatory but if you have any lingering questions they would be birth control pills. We are done breeding. Mike is going to make that decision permanent with a little snipity snip eventually. These two very different types of medicine coexist on the same shelf in the medicine cabinet so that if I see one, I will remember the other. Both have very important yet separate purposes.

I exchanged the bottle of sleepy time goodness for the pink, round disc and then began to work that little pill out of the package. How it works is that you push on the clear front of the package where the pill is, which results in the tiny pill popping through the foil and out the back of the package. I pushed on the little pill pocket, and no pill. Nothing came out the other side. I had been working by nightlight because I am not a fan of the brightness of artificial light. I looked at the front of the dispenser and saw that the pill was stuck. It was lodged crookedly, and did not want to budge. I pushed a little bit harder on the front. No movement.

While the longest sigh ever left my lips, I decided to bang it on the half wall that separates our toilet from the sinks. I gave that baby a couple smacks and the pill popped right out. Not only did it pop out, it performed a triple loop and then flipped into my glass of water. If I was judging the drive based on creativity and least likely place to land in the entire bathroom, yet most likely to land there based upon my day, it would be a stellar ten card I would reveal. If the toilet lid would have been up, then that would have been its final resting place. I just *know* it!

I grabbed the clear glass and saw it resting on the bottom of the water. It was still solid; just sitting there; minding its own business. I thought my chances of fishing it out of the glass were pretty darn good. My pointer finger made the journey through the water and towards the little blue pill. No sudden movements. Slow and steady. That's the way baby. Almost there… The tip of my finger was just about to reach under the tiny blue disc and lift it to the surface. The moment we made contact, finger to pharmaceutical, it turned into mush in the very bottom of my glass. Blue, irretrievable mush. Are you kidding me? *Are you kidding me?!?*

White flag. I surrender!

I set the glass on the counter and set my feet in motion towards my bed. I grabbed my feather pillow, placed it over my face as I reclined back onto the comforter; perpendicular to the bed with my feet dangling off the side.

It felt as if minutes passed as I worked my lungs to fill with air to capacity. I did this before letting out the most generous, resounding, ear piercing shriek that has left my lips in a very, very long time. I had not lost all my marbles. I had the forethought to actually cover my mouth before yelling. That would be one of the gems that I have stored away in my memory from my mom's anecdotal life lessons. She has told me the story several times. It was pertaining to the time she forgot to place a pillow over mouth before screaming at the top of her newly wedded lungs in frustration at my father. She had no idea why she was mad. Could've been his lack of top on the toothpaste or bad toilet aim. Newlywed bliss… If memory serves, this yell resulted in a visit from the neighbors who worried that he was stuffing her into a suitcase to dump her remains into the Wabash River.

I wished someone would stuff my stinking day in a suitcase and float it down a stream to meet up with the sewage it had become. Every time I thought it was going to take a turn for the better, it seemed to go to the dark side. What did I do today to stay on the naughty list?

And if you are worried that this little medicinal mishap has resulted in bouncing baby fertility news that I wanted to share with you, understand this… that would have sent me straight to

195

the straight-jacket! God bless the fact that I had six pills left to swallow and Mike would be gone for ten more days on this trip. Simple math dictates life is good.

The Rose Goes on the Outside

I was absolutely done. I felt like this day had me licked. As I told you before, I am usually the glass half full, happy-go-lucky-girl; but this day, I had met my match. Life had me by the throat and was calling the shots. If I could just get on my jammies and hit the pillow without another incident, then this day would be on its way out and the new one just a few snores away.

I grabbed my pajamas from the dresser and walked back into the bathroom. It was at this moment that I realized that I couldn't remember having peed all day. You know that teachers have to budget their time wisely, and it is really not that unusual in our professional community to reach the late night hours; the end of the day, and realize you never entered the bathroom once. Not once all day! Who has time? We are just thankful that we have bladders of steel!

I sat down on the white porcelain, rested my forehead in my hands with elbows on knees and just spaced out. This was the weirdest of days that I had *ever* been wrapped up in. *Ever.* Is there really a finish line in sight? Is there really rest for the weary, because I feel as if Rip Van Winkle and I could be tight buds and hibernators?

With bladder empty, I stood up to pull up my underwear when the little pink rose caught my eye. The small floret was on the inside of my panties and not on the outside. The stitching was on the outside, and not in where it should be.

Oh...my...gosh!!! I have been wearing my panties inside out all day!

From the moment that I got dressed this morning, this is why I have had one of *the* most cantankerous 24 hours of my life. Could *this* be the explanation for so many of the antics of my day? This entire day I have felt as if something was a bit off, and then it hit me like an epiphany of brilliance. I am Gwyneth!

Did you see the movie <u>Sliding Doors</u> with Gwyneth Paltrow? Oh my gosh, so get this… The movie follows her in two scenarios. She is trying to make it on time her commuter train at the end of a long day. The story line revolves around what happens to her if she *made* the train, and then her life as a result of *missing* the train. Loved it! Brilliant! Go rent it please.

It is that inevitable question of life set in motion by a circumstance, and how the result of said circumstance leaves us on the other side. If she made the train, she gets home just in time to catch her boyfriend cheating on her and cuts him loose. She goes on to live a vibrant life. However, if she misses the train, she remains with this dud of a man and her future goes in a different direction.

That is powerful to me.

What a difference missing a train can make! You either get up the gumption to find the strength to leave the dead weight behind and move on, or you stay in the mundane and day-to-day channels of life and just exist.

All because of timing.

All because you just missed a train.

All because you made the train, just in time.

All because you wore your panties inside out.

I kicked my underwear off, flipped them right side out, by golly and put those panties back on. If it is indeed a theology that I buy into, that my directionally challenged panties wreaked havoc upon my day, it was not going to continue for another

199

moment. *I knew it!* I knew something was just so wrong and I was failed by a wardrobe malfunction of mass proportions today.

I put on my soft, grey jersey knit pants and one of Mike's Purdue shirts and jumped in bed. I looked at the clock which was about 90 minutes shy of Cinderella losing a glass slipper, and was wide-eyed. I could not shake this thought about the "sliding doors" of my day.

My thoughts went from *if the tag would have been on the inside of my panties where it belonged, rather than outside where it soooooo did not belong, what would my day have been like,* to wrestling with the notion that something like wearing your panties inside out can even impact your life at all. If I thought that the state of my clothes dictated my life path, then would I have really made some of the choices in the 80's that I had as far as garments were concerned?

I wore a maroon sweater tie for God's sake! I spent hours using Sun In with my hair dryer while putting on electric blue mascara. And if you think the 90's were much better, there is a photo circulating somewhere in the underbelly of the world with me wearing black MC Hammer pants! That could not have been a good look for me.

Yet those moments of glamour did not lead me to a life on the streets, trying to score more Salon Selectives in a dark alley. Nor did they lead me to live a life of a nuclear scientist rather than the educator and writer that I became. Clothes do not make the man!

So then I flopped over to the thought of God being in control of all things. This would include skivvies facing the right direction right? So was this day really about the directional change of my bloomers, or was it a way to me to evaluate how I handle myself on stranger than strange days. As the last hour of the day settles in, I realize I was definitely challenged. At least directionally challenged below the waist. It happens!

Rather than going to bed all crabby at myself, or the events and people in my day, I went to bed laughing and thinking about how I interacted in each of the moments that made me want to die a slow death by chocolate.

How did I handle myself? Was I a total nut ball? Did my children want to trade me in for a newer, cooler model? That little gift of free will that we were given in the Garden of Eden also refers to not paying close attention to the process when you get dressed in the morning. Again, just as I do not think God is keeping close tabs on the Superman franchise in theaters, nor do I think that He does anything but laugh with me on days like this one.

Notice I said laugh *with* me, not *at* me. Big difference. God has a sense of humor. He truly does! Have you seen a platypus? Ever tried to scratch that little spot between your shoulder blades and twisted, contorted all about to get there and couldn't? Have you ever wondered why when your windshield wipers are clearing the rain they leave a little triangle behind that never clears? I am telling you… GOD WANTS YOU TO LAUGH!

Would I have laughed at the end of this day had I not seen the little rose staring back at me? Probably not. Who knew I needed that kind of laugh today? God did. He knew what kind of day I would have before my feet hit the floor that morning. If you can't laugh at yourself wearing your panties inside out, or whatever your misstep in life might be, then seriously you need to rent a clown suit and simmer down.

The

End

For the Curious

So I might have left you a little curious as to how I made it through Mike's overseas trip. I am happy to report he managed to stay off the terrorist no-fly list. He has traveled quite a bit more since writing about my debacle with my drawers. Many trips have passed us by where some were long, and some short.

My children and I have learned to survive each other when he's gone on trips. I always do a panty double take before putting pants on each morning. My dogs have not escaped again to the blueberry farm, and Ella Gracie is usually found wearing only Hello Kitty boots and panties in their entirety in our home to this day, as you might anticipate.

My silverware is still missing. I never found it while unpacking the garage. Nancy has not been detained for any touchy feely TSA interludes to my knowledge. Jocelyn still reminds me that I have the daughter I asked for and I love every minute of it. Wil has decided that instead of playing golf in high school, like he has trained for since a wee lad, he wants to bowl that round, three hole-drilled sphere down the alley toward ten taunting pins. Anyone want some nice golf clubs?

Ryan has decided to give up his walk-on football career at Purdue to trade it in for the lights and laughter of theater. He is in it for the chicks. His words, not mine.

My dad is doing well. He still bleeds black and gold. My mom got a new knee this spring, and God love her she has been called THE BEST rehabbing patient that has bounced back from this type of overhaul her therapists have seen. Don't tell her this, but I think the therapists say that to everyone! She is motivated by traveling with my dad to Ireland while he is on sabbatical from Purdue. I call it bribery! I think she'll make it.

Let's cut to the fat shall we? The real information you are looking for is the score of Henry vs. butter:

Henry 6 and ½

Butter ½

The half that survived his chompers was a mini stick that he had tried to devour on the kitchen counter, but ended up knocking it off the plate and behind the toaster while we were at church one Sunday. Viva la beurre!

Margie and I had breakfast just this morning for my birthday. Even though the big four-oh hit the calendar in January for me, I am one who embraces birthdays not shuns them, so we celebrated today, and it is never to be called belated. My celebration lasts 364 days! We ate at Route 66 and I looked for that sweet couple that I have seen there several times enjoying the paper during the year, but they must not dine there on Wednesday mornings. I was sad not to see them. I had hoped to tell you more about them.

And then there is me. I am doing ok. I am at a place in life where I am trying to listen more and speak less. I have a lot to say so that listening piece can be hard for me at times. I am working on choosing to say "No" even to good things sometimes when my plate is full. Again, harder for me than you could possibly know.

I am still contemplating placement of the tattoo I yearn for. I talked with a friend this winter who lives in Miami and told him I was ready, after 10 years of talking about it to get inked. Understand that because I have been talking about this tat for ten years, Mike thinks it will never happen. This same friend showed me one he had placed on his calf of the ladybug from the Pixar movie *A Bug's Life* and said that it was in honor of his wife. I told him I was going to get one too, not of a ladybug mind you, but that I wanted a tattoo of the infinity symbol and also my children's initials morphed into some kind of thing that when you look at the parts and not the whole, you see their respective initials. My problem is that I want it placed where it will hurt the least and I am deathly worried it will be my forehead. He told me to "get over it because no matter where you get ink, it hurts!" Good advice Tim. Good advice.

But wait...want more?

 You can check in on Jen and find out what is happening with her latest news and events:

Princesswithapen.com

Follow her on Twitter: authorjentucker

Facebook: Jen Tucker and Author Jen Tucker

Other books by Writing Career Coach Press

The Road To Acceptance

ISBN: 978-0-9833607-5-9

From the time I was a child I sought a God who loved me just as I was. I found the all-caring God and Savior, Jesus Christ when I was 27 years old, in a moment of despair, coming off of alcohol, speed and marijuana. I finally began living a life worth living, a life worthy of my Jesus dying on the Cross. I now know that whoever you are, whatever you've done, Jesus is waiting for you to come back to His arms, stains and all. This is the story of my journey seeking and finding the Lord of Lords, Jesus Christ.

Earning a Living as a Writer (Workbook) - *Available Now!*

ISBN: 978-0-9833607-4-2

Do you have a story to share? Do you want to earn an income as a writer? The world of publishing is changing. E-books & Small presses are on the rise. It is easier to get your book published, but harder to make a living with publishing. What is an aspiring writer to do?

You need to remember the fundamentals & adjust them to the changing market. What are Blogs, Vlogs, Trailers, Pitches, Hooks, Blurbs, & Platforms? And what in the WORLD do they have to do with writing? How can you get your writing in front of the right people without doing the WRONG things? Are you ready to reach your goals, or even your dreams? When publishers were offering smaller cash advances & magazines were disappearing from shelves, my company tripled its gross revenue. In this course I want to help you create a plan to reach your writing goals. This Workbook is designed to be used with the audio lessons of the same name.

Watch for the book version! Coming late Summer 2011!

CPSIA information can be obtained at www.ICGtesting.com
Printed in the USA
LVOW040425130911

245970LV00001B/3/P